LIFE – AND HOW TO THINK ABOUT IT

THE NO–NONSENSE GUIDE TO A THOUGHTFUL LIFE

Richard Docwra is a writer, coach and consultant. He's produced books, guides, podcasts and other publications on a wide range of topics including politics, philosophy and what makes people tick. His books include 'The Life Trap' and 'Modern life – as good as it gets?', and his articles have appeared in a range of magazines and websites.

Richard also provides consultancy to organisations and movements seeking to change the world for the better. He is the founder and director of social change agency ChangeStar, as well as the not-for-profit organisation Life Squared, which helps people navigate the complexity of life so they can live in a happier, wiser and more meaningful way.

Visit www.lifesquared.org.uk to access lots of free resources from Richard and the team.

BY

RICHARD DOCWRA

BOOKS

The Life Trap

Modern Life - as Good as it Gets?

BOOKLETS

Living Well

How to eat and exercise well

Manifesto for life

How to be civilised

How to be alone (and not lonely)

How to think about death (and life)

How to achieve less

The story of energy

How to have a better Christmas

The modern life survival guide

The problem with consumerism

The Amazing (how to find peak experience in everyday life)

How to live ethically

LIFE – AND HOW TO THINK ABOUT IT

THE NO-NONSENSE GUIDE TO A THOUGHTFUL LIFE

For Izzy – *wishing you a happy and thoughtful life.*

First published in Great Britain in 2021 by Big
Idea Publishing

Big Idea Publishing is a trading name of
Docwra Ltd

Registered Office: Lewes House,
32 High Street, Lewes, E Sussex BN7 2LX

Company Registration Number No. 7793032

www.richarddocwra.com

@RichardDocwra

Design by Richard Slade.
Typeset in 11 on 14 point Century Schoolbook

A CIP catalogue record for this book is available
from the British Library.

ISBN 978-1-8383396-0-9

eISBN 978-1-8383396-1-6

CONTENTS

INTRODUCTION

"What is the point of this book?"

This is the question you may be asking yourself as you open these pages.

You may be someone who rolls along through life reasonably happily, or you may struggle with some of the challenges that life presents us to us all. Whatever your experience of life or outlook on it, you may also feel you have some unanswered questions. Perhaps you may have briefly posed these to yourself or mulled them over when you've had some time on your own but never really explored them in detail. These may include 'What is the meaning of life?', 'How did we get here?' and 'What happens when I die?'.

The aim of this book is to help you explore some of these bigger questions, and demonstrate that these are some of the most important things we can think about. Thinking about these issues is not only incredibly interesting, but can also have a profound and positive effect on your life. For example, it can give you a broader perspective on the world and open up possibilities that you never knew existed. Overall, it can help you adopt a better-informed approach to life and make the most of the short time that each of us has on this planet.

Think of this book as a 'map' for life that you could use if you found yourself waking up somewhere strange and unfamiliar as a human being for the first time and had to start finding your way around and making the most of the time you had there.

This is of course the situation that we're all faced with when we're born, although most of us aren't lucky enough to have a comprehensive map to help us navigate life. Instead, each of us is unceremoniously dumped onto a planet, without any choice in the matter, not knowing where we are, who we are or why we're here. We then spend much of the lifetime that follows trying to make sense of these questions.

I believe that people need to be given the opportunity, tools and support to start considering these questions earlier on in life. They need to be seen as a fundamental part of our education, both in our childhood, and throughout life. Because this stuff matters. If we can't navigate life effectively, we may not end up living the lives we could have done, or being the compassionate and civilised creatures that we could be.

When we are young, a massive stretch of unknown territory stands before us in life, with countless possible paths of how we could behave, what we could believe and what we could do with our life. Most of us (if we are lucky) are shown a few specific footpaths by parents, teachers and other sources, but there are no formal institutions or services in society that help us take a real 'bird's eye view' of life and really consider the path we want to take.

To continue this analogy, the footpaths we are given by other people can be useful, but might also take us down some paths that we may not want to go down in our lives. Surely we'd prefer to think for ourselves about the paths we wish to follow?

We spend most of our lives trampling through the undergrowth and labouring along paths we've not chosen for ourselves, which may not be the right ones for us. This is a particular issue in a world that is now more complex than ever before, where there are more possible paths than ever, and many powerful sources of influence (from advertisers to newspapers) trying to make us take particular paths, which is often for their benefit rather than ours.

So, the aim of this book is to give you a map for life. Something that will help you rise above the detail of your daily concerns and the paths you've been treading, and get some broader perspective on life and what's out there. A map you can return to whenever you're in need of direction.

This book doesn't specifically deal with day-to-day matters like how to be a good parent or how to make a great omelette but it does provide you with a set of broader tools to help you navigate life. These should give you a solid foundation to help inform your approach to smaller, more practical issues.

This book has been written for someone like me. Someone who is not an intellectual but is curious about the world and wants to make sense of some of the bigger questions so that they can live a better-informed and more fulfilled life. The book aims to be interesting, accessible and no-nonsense. You don't need an understanding of philosophy to enjoy this book and it's not going to be sniffy or condescending towards the beliefs you hold. But it will hopefully challenge them and get you to think about them in a more rigorous way.

The book is structured into ten specific 'big questions' that people might ask about life - from 'How can I find meaning in my life?' to 'How should I behave?'. In each of chapters we'll explore a range of topics to help you shed some light on each big question.

You won't necessarily receive a final, concrete answer to each question but as you read through the book you'll be going through the process of thinking about them for yourself. So you should hopefully reach the end of each chapter (and the book) with a better sense of where you stand on each question, as well as with the tools to think about it in more detail should you wish. There are some suggestions for further reading at the end of the book to help you go deeper into each question if you'd like to.

So, open up your map and let's see where we are!

Richard Docwra, September 2020

LIFE – IN A NUTSHELL

The universe is a vast collection of minute subatomic particles. You are a collection of some of these particles that have coalesced together for a brief period into a form we describe as a human being. You are a medium-sized creature living on the planet Earth - a small planet in a solar system surrounding just one of billions of stars within the Milky Way galaxy, itself one of 10 billion galaxies in the known universe.

You will be alive for up to around 80 years, during which you temporarily have the capacity to experience a range of sensory inputs and emotions and undertake abstract thought. It is up to you what attitude you take to being alive, and how you choose to make the most of this time. It is also up to you to find out what gives you meaning in life.

Before and after this period of being alive, you, and your thoughts, memories and sense of self, simply won't exist. Seeing life like this - as a temporary period of existing; an opportunity to be grabbed - can help us appreciate it more, as well as help us deal better with some of the things people tend to fear most while they are alive - including the end of life.

You will get more out of life if you approach it with a sense of curiosity and try to live in a well-informed way. This includes getting some perspective on your situation as a creature by asking questions such as 'Where am I?', 'What am I?' and 'What is the reality I live within?'.

We each create our own meaning in life, but many people share quite similar ideas of what gives them meaning. Many of the things that matter most in our lives are quite simple and right in front of our eyes - from nature to the people we love - and yet we often don't appreciate them enough as we're busy seeking other things that don't matter so much.

This is because we're not entirely rational creatures, even though we might think we are. Human beings are prone to traits in thinking and behaviour, including conforming with others and comparing our situation in relation to others, that can make us vulnerable to influence from other people - from advertisers to groups of friends.

You will grow up surrounded by lots of people, institutions and ideas - from your parents to religions through to the economic system you live within - that will try to influence you to live, think or behave in particular ways.

If you are to be free and truly live your own life, you need to learn how to think for yourself in the face of all these influences, in order to challenge them and choose the ideas, values and way of life that truly suit you - not those that have been pedalled to you. Collectively, these thinking skills could be called 'life literacy', and this book aims to help you start building them.

While you are alive, you will also need to consider how your behaviour affects the other people, creatures and environment around you. This isn't always easy to do well, so it helps to have a clear idea of what our values are and to think about how we can most effectively live in line with them.

As a human being, you are neither 'good' nor 'bad' (as these things don't really exist) but, because of your tendency towards certain traits of thinking and behaviour, you can behave in ways that are both consistent with your moral values and that aren't, depending on the values you pick up in life and the situations you find yourself in. You, like other humans, are capable of acts of extreme kindness and sacrifice, but also acts of savage, unthinking cruelty.

Most people share some similar basic values (such as compassion, kindness and fairness), but we need to build a society that reflects these and makes it easy to uphold them.

As you go through life and time passes, many things will change, including your ideas, friends and physical condition. It will make your life better if you can learn to accept the changes you experience that you can't control. This will enable you to be at peace with yourself, your life and your death. It will also help you to get more from the short time you have to be alive.

Overall, you will get much more out of life if you live it in a considered, well-informed way. This book helps you start this process.

FINDING YOUR BEARINGS

CHAPTER 1
THE POWER OF KNOWLEDGE

Why perspective matters —
The power of accumulated knowledge

The first question you might ask yourself as you seek to navigate your way through life is 'Where am I?'.

During our lives, we take a lot of things for granted, and our place within the bigger picture is one of them. Most people realise they are a human being living on Earth and that our planet is part of a wider universe. But many people don't have much of a picture beyond these basic facts.

There is a much deeper understanding available to us of our position as individual creatures with particular abilities, limitations and tendencies. Developing this understanding can help us live richer and better-informed lives. The first part of this book aims to help you build this deeper sense of what you are and your position in the greater scheme of things, as well as what this means for your life.

To help us build this picture, we need to gain perspective on our lives. This means standing back and seeing a situation in a wider context. It is a thinking skill that can be extremely useful when we are immersed in any form of complexity – from thinking about our existence as a human being through to battling with a moral question.

We can get perspective on any topic, but to inform our lives in the modern world we need to develop perspective across a particular range of topics, including our makeup as living organisms, our situation in relation to other people around the world, and the systems and ideas we use to govern our lives.

WHY PERSPECTIVE MATTERS

In order to develop perspective on these topics, we need to learn about them in a particular way.

There is a massive amount of information and knowledge available to us in the modern world, and it is impossible for one person to have anything approaching a comprehensive knowledge of every topic.

We therefore need to develop our knowledge of the world around us in the same way as we would use a map. Maps work because they sacrifice detail (e.g. an exact description of the surroundings in a particular location, such as the colour of the flowers) in order to provide an overall perspective. They focus on the most important information that will enable users to achieve a particular aim - in the case of a map, to find their way around the terrain represented on it.

We can take the same approach to learning about the world around us. In this way of learning, understanding the overall structure and parameters of a topic is just as important as understanding some of the detail, as this overview enables us to find our way around it and then seek further information on a particular area should we wish. For example, rather than learning in detail about every King and Queen of England, it might be more useful to start by learning about the different ways of governing a country, and how England ended up with a monarchy.

Even abstract ideas such as 'morality' have parameters and structure to them that people can learn about, and use to help them navigate specific moral views and arguments more effectively. So, in this book, we'll aim to gain perspective on a range of topics - from ideas like morality through to the beliefs we hold about the world around us - so that we can navigate life better.

There are many benefits of gaining a sense of perspective on our lives within the great scheme of things. It can help you get more out of the experience of living, and be less prone to anxiety or fear of things you don't understand.

For example, if you can picture your own life within the context of the larger universe and the wider flow of history, you can emerge with a sense that you are reasonably insignificant yet extraordinarily lucky to have the chance to experience life. This can provide you with a range of positive thoughts to carry through daily life, including a sense of comfort that, whatever the trials and tribulations of your own life, you are part of something much bigger. It can also provide an injection of energy, enthusiasm and wonder into every day of being alive. It is also a form of wisdom, as among many other things, it enables us to understand ourselves better, react in a more balanced way to the highs and lows of life and view other people in a more understanding way.

A second benefit of perspective is that it can help us to better understand various major aspects of our lives and the world. As a consequence, it can help us to navigate our way through life more easily, both on large questions and everyday ones. For example, it can help us to consider big questions such as what gives us meaning in our lives. It can then also aid our decision-making about more detailed, everyday issues such as 'should I move town to take this new job or stay where my friends are?'.

The manifold disadvantages of not possessing perspective can be taken to be the reverse of each of the points above – for example, having an unrealistic view of the world or your own situation as a creature, getting stressed or confused by the apparent complexity of the world and making poor decisions in life.

In short, without a sense of perspective, our awareness of life will be as restricted as our view of the world might be if we were sitting in the middle of a forest without a map. Our path through life is also likely to be just as random and uninformed as our path through the forest would be, and we would have little knowledge to give us any comfort about our place within the 'bigger picture'. The solution in both situations is the same – we need to 'lift ourselves above' the position we find ourselves in, and gain perspective on it. We do this by increasing our knowledge of certain aspects of the world around us, using a map.

THE POWER OF ACCUMULATED KNOWLEDGE

Perhaps the most important factor in our development as a species (aside from the environment that keeps us alive) has been our ability to communicate and pass on knowledge to each other. Not just passing this knowledge between individuals, but down the generations, for perpetuity.

As the psychologist Professor Bruce Hood notes, "we are the only animals on this planet that retain skills and knowledge to pass on to our offspring."[1]

Over millennia, human beings have learnt to accumulate knowledge in this way through telling stories to each other and, more recently, passing knowledge down through writing and other methods.

Doing this has enabled us to learn. We would not have the modern world without this ability. Accumulating knowledge has enabled us to achieve countless things - from identifying which foods are poisonous through to building solid, warm houses and sending people safely into space.

1   Hood, Bruce - The Self Illusion, Constable, London 2012, p.26

If we didn't have this ability, we'd repeat the same mistakes - some of which would be fatal. Life and civilization would not move on. Life would be hard, and short. The value of accumulated knowledge is enormous - but could be summarised as:

- Reducing suffering
- Making our lives longer
- Improving the lives of more people and other creatures.

As you build this knowledge (through learning and reading), you give yourself a more solid foundation on which to build your life and a clearer perspective through which to see the world. In turn, you give yourself the potential for a richer, more fulfilling and longer life.

This accumulated knowledge has come at a significant cost. Many people and other creatures have died and suffered in helping us to build this knowledge, and it has taken years of substantial investment and sacrifice to accrue. It therefore makes sense to take advantage of this wonderful, priceless resource.

ACTION

KEEP LEARNING

See learning as a wonderful, priceless resource that you are privileged to have access to. Make it part of your aim every day to be curious and learn something new. You can learn in a variety of ways - from conversation to reading, through to exploring.

Now, let us start building some perspective and learning about where you are.

CHAPTER 2

WHERE AM I?

Where you are — Your place in history — The modern world

WHERE YOU ARE

Our sense of 'where we are' in the great scheme of things and the reality that we are living in is simply an interpretation - in other words, a model of that reality. It is based on what we experience through our senses, as well as ideas and stories that we have developed as a species to represent that reality. We will discuss this more in chapter 3. The best interpretation we have of this reality is as follows.

We live on a small planet, orbiting a medium-sized sun that sits in a solar system within a galaxy within a universe.

The universe is massive. In fact, it's so large that it can be difficult for us to comprehend, as the scale is so much greater than anything we're used to imagining. Let's start with our own solar system and work outwards from there.

OUR SOLAR SYSTEM

We live on the third planet away from the Sun in our solar system.

Most of the models or pictures you will have seen of the solar system fail to give an accurate impression of its scale - simply because it is so large. Here is a quick thought experiment (borrowed with thanks from NOAO) to illustrate the scale of the solar system.

Imagine the Earth (8,000 miles wide in reality) is the size of a peppercorn. At this scale, the Sun (800,000 miles wide) is about the size of a bowling ball (8 inches).

- The first planet from the Sun - Mercury - will be the size of a pinhead, 10 yards away from the Sun.
- The second planet - Venus, will be the size of a peppercorn, 19 yards away from the Sun.
- Earth, the third planet, will also be the size of a peppercorn, 26 yards away from the Sun.
- Mars, the fourth planet, is the size of a pinhead, 40 yards away from the Sun.
- Jupiter is the size of a chestnut, 135 yards from the Sun.
- Saturn is smaller, the size of an acorn, 247 yards from the Sun.
- The seventh planet, Uranus, is the size of a peanut, 496 yards from the Sun.
- The eighth planet, Neptune, is also the size of a peanut, 777 yards from the Sun - nearly half a mile away, even at this scale.

And just in case that hasn't blown your mind, here's one final thing to consider. If the Earth was the size of a grain of sand, our solar system (out to the planet Neptune) would be as big as a cathedral.

OUR GALAXY

Nearly all the stars we can see with the naked eye are in our galaxy, the Milky Way. Our Sun is just one of at least 100 billion stars in our galaxy, most of which have their own planets and solar systems too.

The Milky Way is a spiral galaxy, and according to NASA, "the stars are arranged in a pinwheel pattern with four major arms, and we live about two-thirds of the way up one of them."[2]

The nearest star to the Sun, Proxima Centuri, is 40,000,000,000,000 (forty trillion) kilometers away. To make sense of these vast distances, astronomers measure distance using 'light years' - one light year being the distance light can travel in one year. This is about 9,000,000,000,000 kilometers - so Proxima Centuri is around 4.2 light years away.

Our galaxy is about 100,000 light years across. So, if our solar system was the size of a grain of sand, our galaxy would be 1,000 times bigger than a cathedral.

So that's just the size of our own galaxy. When you look beyond this, things get truly mind-boggling.

OUR UNIVERSE

The nearest galaxy to ours is the Andromeda galaxy. This is around 2.5 million light years away.

The visible universe (the universe that we can see with the aid of the best telescopes) contains around 10 billion (10,000,000,000) galaxies. Each one of those galaxies contains around 100 billion (10,000,000,000) stars.

So, the visible universe contains 10,000 billion (10,000,000,0 00,000,000,000,000) stars. There are more stars in the universe than there are grains of sand on our planet.

The visible universe stretches around 13 billion light years from the Earth. So, let's now put the overall scale of the universe

---

2   solarsystem.nasa.gov/solar-system/beyond/in-depth/

into context - and even using objects we can recognise, the scale is hard to comprehend:

- If the Earth was the size of a grain of sand, our solar system (out to the planet Neptune) would be as big as a cathedral.
- Then, if our solar system were the size of a grain of sand, our galaxy would be 1,000 times bigger than a cathedral.
- Finally, if our galaxy were the size of a grain of sand, the visible universe would be as big as a cathedral.

ACTION

YOU AND THE UNIVERSE

Once you've read the information about the universe above, take a few minutes to reflect on it. What is your reaction to the scale of the universe? How does it make you feel about yourself and your life? How does it make you want to live?

OUR PLANET

Planet Earth has a circumference of about 24,901 miles (40,075 km).

Nearly 70 percent of the planet's surface is covered by water. Earth's global ocean "has an average depth of about 2.5 miles (4 kilometers) and contains 97 percent of Earth's water."[3]

Earth is surrounded by an atmosphere, the bulk of which extends from the Earth's surface up to about 5-9 miles above it[4]. This thin band is essential for life and is the place in which we, and all other life, dwell.

---

3   solarsystem.nasa.gov/planets/earth/in-depth
4   www.nationalgeographic.org/encyclopedia/atmosphere-RL

OUR PLANET SUPPORTS LIFE

According to BBC Science, "Earth's distance from the Sun is thought to be one of the key reasons why it is home to widespread life. Our planet occupies what scientists sometimes call the Goldilocks zone. Its distance from our star means it is neither too hot, nor too cold to support liquid water - thought to be a key ingredient for life. Astronomers are searching for rocky planets like ours in the Goldilocks zones of other stars."

Our planet, Earth, is currently the only planet known to support life in the universe, although it is quite possible that others do too, given the scale of the universe and the known existence of other planets in the Goldilocks zones of other stars.

WHAT IS LIFE?

This is a harder question to answer than you might think, and there is currently no agreed consensus on the definition of 'life'. Some scientists argue that it is a mistake to try to define 'life', as what they are interested in is understanding the nature of our world, rather than trying to chip away at a definition of it to fit our language. This may seem like an obscure point but it's an important one about the reality we live within and our attempts as human beings to describe it using our limited experience of this reality and the limited language we have available. We'll explore this further in a later chapter.

A simple scientific definition of life might read something like this: "the condition that distinguishes organisms from inorganic objects and dead organisms, being manifested by growth through metabolism, reproduction, and the power of adaptation to environment through changes originating internally."[5]

In chapter 4 we'll go beyond this biological definition of life, to also consider life as an idea - specifically, your own life.

5   www.dictionary.com/browse/life

LIFE ON EARTH

There are about 8.7 million species of living thing on Earth - with 6.5 million of these on land and 2.2 million in the oceans.

This is of course a rough figure, but it's the best one we have. We have only catalogued about 1.2 million of these species, and it would take another 480 years to catalogue the rest, so scientists have tried to predict the total number from the one already known.[6] Many of the species in the estimated total have simply not been discovered yet.

Every one of these species evolved from a single organism that lived around 3.5 billion years ago.[7]

This remarkable insight was first put forward by Charles Darwin in the nineteenth century, who (at the same time as his lesser-known counterpart Alfred Russel Wallace) proposed the theory of evolution. This has become our most credible explanation of how life on Earth has developed over time.

HOW WE PERCEIVE SCALE

As we've already seen, the universe in which we live is massive compared to our size as human beings. But there is an equally awe-inspiring scale of smaller things.

If you were to take a small object, like a grape, and try to break it down into its smallest component parts, you'd eventually see molecules, which are made of atoms bound up together. Educator Jonathan Butterworth takes up the story from here:

"A molecule is the smallest unit of any chemical compound. An atom is the smallest unit of any element in the periodic table. But the atom is not the smallest unit of matter. Experiments found that each atom has a tiny, dense nucleus, surrounded by a cloud of even tinier electrons. Matter is made of fundamental particles, the smallest things in the universe. Particles interact with each other according to a theory called the "Standard Model". The

6 www.nature.com/articles/news.2011.498
7 www.nationalgeographic.com/news/2010/5/100513-science-evolution-darwin-single-ancestor

Standard Model is a remarkably elegant encapsulation of the strange quantum world of indivisible, infinitely small particles. It also covers the forces that govern how particles move, interact, and bind together to give shape to the world around us."[8]

We live in a reality with extremes of scale that are almost too much for our minds to comprehend. Day to day we just tend to judge things on a scale that's relevant to us - the medium-sized stuff we can see on or just above the surface of the planet. Anything much smaller or larger than this we ignore. This is a reasonable strategy as these are the things that are likely to affect us and our survival most.

But it can be useful to regularly stand back from our everyday 'bubble' and get some perspective to see the extremes of both large and small scales that we live within.

We could probably argue that we're medium-sized creatures in relation to the other living things on our planet. The largest animal in the world is the Blue Whale, which has a largest recorded weight of 190 tons and can be the size of a jumbo jet. The smallest mammal is the Etruscan shrew, weighing less than 3 grams and the size of a paper clip.[9]

ACTION

THE WORLD BENEATH YOUR FEET

You've reflected on your life within the bigger scale - and you can do the same for the smaller scale. Find a patch of grass, and kneel or lie on it on your front. Put your face close to the ground, peel back the grass and take a look at the tiny world and lives being led below it. Reflect on the fact that ours is not the only scale of world in which lives are being lived.

8   www.ted.com/talks/jonathan_butterworth_what_s_the_smallest_thing_in_
     the_universe/transcript?language=en
9   www.britannica.com/list/queen-mabs-stable-7-of-the-smallest-animals

YOUR PLACE IN HISTORY

Scientists believe the universe was formed 13.7 billion years ago in the Big Bang. The planet Earth was formed around 4.5 billion years ago.

The first microscopic life appeared on Earth 3.7 billion years ago, and a vast amount of time passed before animals evolved to appear on land around 400 million years ago.

You are a member of the species homo sapiens, and your species evolved around only 200,000 years ago - a flicker in the overall life of the planet and the species that have lived on it. As the great Carl Sagan noted, if the history of the universe was compressed into one year, human beings and all of human history would only have been around for the last 10 seconds.

A key turning point in the development of human societies was around 12,000 years when "humans found they could control the growth and breeding of certain plants and animals. This discovery led to farming and herding animals, activities that transformed Earth's natural landscapes—first locally, then globally.

As humans invested more time in producing food, they settled down. Villages became towns, and towns became cities. With more food available, the human population began to increase dramatically."[10] Many of the key developments in human history like this that we take for granted have taken place reasonably recently.

The last 200 or so years of human history have featured some even more rapid changes and development in science and technology (from the discovery of electricity to the invention of the motor car) that have changed the way we understand the world and live our lives.

These changes have also had a significant impact on our planet. From the massive increase in our use of the planet's natural resources through to the development of urban areas, roads and agriculture to service the rapidly growing human

10   humanorigins.si.edu/human-characteristics/humans-change-world

population, these changes have threatened some of the other estimated 8.7 million species that live on Earth.

THE MODERN WORLD

In this section we will explore some of the main features of life in the modern world and some of the dominant ideas overarching us. Naturally, both of these lists are very brief and non-exhaustive, as the world is a big place with a lot of diversity. There will be different features, ideas and stories according to the country you live in, your culture, religion and even family background. In this section we will simply look at some of the key features and dominant ideas in what we know as the western world.

Before we begin, let us briefly pause to consider the importance and influence of ideas. We cannot explore the history of human beings without looking at the history of the ideas we've developed that have shaped our lives, values and societies.

As human beings, we are surrounded by ideas that we have made up - including how we should behave, what to believe, how our political system should be structured and what matters in life. People live and die for some of these ideas, and are capable of acts of great kindness and extreme cruelty because of them. We will explore some of these ideas in more detail later in this book.

These ideas come from a wide range of sources, including religions, economic systems, political systems, traditions, cultures, families and so on.

Sometimes, the ideas around us are communicated through the use of stories. We use stories to understand and explain the world and our place in it, as well as to gain power over people, access resources and organise our societies. These stories include religious ideas, economic principles, political ideas and philosophies of how we should live.

Different periods of human history can be seen to have been dominated by particular ideas and stories, even if these ideas weren't immediately apparent to most of the people living within them at the time. It's vitally important for us to be able to understand some of the key ideas and stories that dominated our past, as they help us understand history better, and could enable us to avoid repeating past mistakes. It's also important for us to recognise the dominant ideas of the age we're living in so that we can challenge them and decide if we want to follow them or not.

Most importantly, it's vital that we understand these ideas are simply made up, arbitrary, invented fictions that are plucked out of the air and survive only by the fact that they are believed (or upheld through being enforced) rather than eternal truths.

By recognising this, we gain a completely new view of the reality that we live within and have been brought up in, as well as the broader possibilities for society and our own lives. We don't have to follow the ideas or stories we're brought up within or that overarch us - we can create our own, better stories. And that is a core part of not just building a better life of your own, but a better society as well. What ideas do you want to have - and what ideas would you like other people to have?

This also helps us challenge people in power - as perhaps one definition of 'power' or 'authority' is the ability to make people follow the ideas and stories you want them to. But if we know that these ideas are made up, and are seeking to follow our own ideas rather than those forced on us then we are exercising our own power and standing up for our freedom.

Now let's consider some of the key characteristics of the modern world, and some of the dominant ideas that influence our lives today.

HEALTH AND LONGEVITY

Human life expectancy has increased enormously in the last couple of centuries. Before the advent of the modern world, life expectancy was around 30 years in all regions of the world.

"Life expectancy has increased rapidly since the Age of Enlightenment. In the early 19th century, life expectancy started to increase in the early industrialized countries while it stayed low in the rest of the world. Since 1900 the global average life expectancy has more than doubled and is now above 70 years."[11]

These changing population demographics, coupled with improvements in our health and quality of life in old age, are now challenging us to look at older age differently - not as a time when our usefulness expires, we fade from society and wait for death, but as another important phase of our lives where we can lead an active, useful and fulfilled existence.

POPULATION GROWTH

Global average life expectancy isn't the only thing that has grown quickly in the last couple of centuries. The global population has too. At around 8,000 BC when agriculture was invented the world population was around 5 million people. To quote Hans Rosling of Gapminder "This number increased only slowly for 10,000 years, eventually reaching 1 billion in the year 1800. Then something happened. The next billion were added in only 130 years. And another 5 billion were added in under 100 years."[12]

We are now at a global population of around 7.7 billion people. The UN forecasts this growth will flatten to a population of around 10-12 billion by the end of this century. So, the massive growth is unlikely to increase forever, as many people fear. There are however real concerns about how the growing human population has affected the global ecosystem and the effects that further growth in the population will bring, from the unsustainable amount of resources we consume to the devastating impact we are having on nature, which according to a recent report by the UN is "declining globally at rates unprecedented in human history – and the rate of species extinctions is accelerating."[13]

11 www.ourworldindata.org/life-expectancy
12 Rosling, Hans, Factfulness, Sceptre, London 2018, p.80
13 www.un.org/sustainabledevelopment/blog/2019/05/nature-decline-unprecedented-report

ENVIRONMENTAL IMPACT

Following from the above point, it is clear we are living beyond the planet's means. And this is not necessarily an issue of population growth - it is about the way we are living in certain parts of the world and the impact this is having on the planet as a result, including the resources we are consuming, the land we are using and the waste we are producing.

For example, if everyone in the world were to maintain a lifestyle similar to that of a typical person in the UK we'd need the equivalent of 2.7 planets. Based on someone in the USA it would be 5 planets. And as we only have one planet, we need to adjust our behaviour.

These aren't just numbers. For decades, our behaviour has had a massive impact on the planet and in recent decades we have been seeing it in front of our eyes. For example, climate change caused by human impact is already causing the planet to warm up, bringing extreme weather, melting glaciers and ice sheets, and threatening a range of catastrophic effects on human populations around the planet if we continue the same behaviour. But climate change is just one example of many negative impacts we are having on our environment.

Overall, it is clear we are facing the biggest challenge humanity as a whole has ever faced - not just how to tackle climate change but how to live within the finite resources of one planet and conserve the ecosystem and biodiversity that is so important for its own sake, whilst maintaining a large (and, for now, growing) human population.

This challenge is made significantly harder for us when you consider the dominant ideas that surround us in the modern world. Our economic and political systems are driven by the desire for ever more economic growth, and our culture is dominated by the idea that travel, consumption and having more material goods are desirable and measurements of your success as a person. Culturally, we prize the idea of individual freedom above almost anything else, yet we face an issue that may require us to regulate our behaviour if we are to address it.

These ideas and beliefs surround us, and are promoted through a range of institutions (including workplaces, careers advice and education) and channels (such as advertising, newspapers and other places). It is therefore very difficult, even though the evidence about the environmental challenges we face is now unavoidable, to turn this massive global ship around when its structure, institutions and values are still ultimately based on ideas that conflict with the idea of living within limits and protecting nature.

To change society on this scale we have to change the ideas that overarch us, into those that prioritise the flourishing of human beings and nature together rather than prioritising economic growth. And this starts with each of us adopting these new ideas.

INEQUALITY

There is inequality among human beings across a range of variables in the modern world, including gender, race and wealth. To illustrate the effects of this inequality, let us look at wealth.

There are big differences in wealth across the global population. The Gross Domestic Product (GDP) per person in the USA is $54,629.50, whereas in Malawi it's $815.10 - a 67-fold difference. In Tanzania, 73% of the population live on less than $2 per day. Inequality also exists within individual countries and communities.

There are also extremes of wealth distribution in the world, with a small number of particularly rich people. For example, 85 of the world's billionaires have the same wealth as the bottom 50% of the world's population.

As a consequence of these variations in people's situations around the world, the possibilities and outcomes of our lives are often determined by the country, culture and family we find ourselves born into.

Just to illustrate this, your life and education prospects will be very different depending on the country you live in. For example, in the UK 98% of children attend primary school, whereas in Chad only 32% of children get this opportunity.

As another example, although average life expectancy across the world has doubled in the last hundred years, and is now around 71 years, "The inequality of life expectancy is still very large across and within countries. In 2019 the country with the lowest life expectancy is the Central African Republic with 53 years, in Japan life expectancy is 30 years longer."[14]

When an individual or group is affected by inequality it can have a profoundly negative impact on every area of their life, and tackling inequality has been a sincere mission for many politicians, organisations, campaigners and other individuals in society over the years.

Human beings have an uneasy relationship with inequality. No-one likes to see other people suffering, but when one is part of a group that benefits from inequality (such as wealthy people, for example), it is very difficult to appreciate the full range of ways in which the inequality negatively affects other people's lives (such as poverty affecting a wide range of factors from health to educational attainment). On a psychological level, it has been shown that losses matter more to human beings than gains, so there may also be a reluctance (conscious or otherwise) on behalf of those with more to give more ground to those with less.

A good example of this is economic inequality. No-one likes to see other people in poverty or in suffering, and there is often great generosity when people are asked to give to others in need. But at the same time, left wing political parties and ideas that seek a more equal distribution of wealth and greater investment in services for all (through higher taxes and other mechanisms) have been considerably less popular in the modern age than those on the right that enable people to keep most of their earnings for themselves and not share this wealth with those who need it.

All of this suggests that fighting inequality is likely to be an ongoing battle for human beings.

14 www.ourworldindata.org/life-expectancy

TECHNOLOGY

Advances in scientific knowledge in the last 500 years, and particularly in computer science in the last 50 years, have transformed the way we live our lives. Human beings are supported by technology in a wide range of aspects of their lives, including food production, medicine, housing, travel and communication.

Being surrounded by this technology - from houses to cities - can make us forget that we are ultimately just another species of animal living in, and dependent on, the natural world.

ACTION

OUR PLACE IN NATURE

Take a moment to imagine what the place you are sitting or standing in would look like without human intervention or technology. You might be standing in a grassy plain, a forest or some other natural environment. Remind yourself that many of the things surrounding you are temporary, artificial inventions and that you are ultimately just part of nature.

COMMUNICATIONS

We live in a world of cheap and almost instant communication, in which people from opposite sides of the world can send information to each other in a split second, at (seemingly) no cost to each other. This speed of communication enables services to function quicker than ever before (such as effectively instant financial transactions), and news to be reported from almost anywhere in the world while events are taking place.

SPEED AND PRODUCTIVITY

At the same time as having the capability to 'go fast', we live in a culture where speed is seen as positive and important. Influences on our current attitudes towards time can be traced back to early Christianity, which not only warned against laziness but also developed a regimented, disciplined attitude towards time – for example, within the codes for monastic living set down within the Rule of Saint Benedict, which was influential in the Church in the Middle Ages. As the power and influence of the Church spread, so did its values.

Perhaps the most obvious influence on our modern attitude towards time was the Industrial Revolution and the advent of industrial capitalism. At this point, industrialists began to see a worker's time in the workplace as a resource to be managed. Efficient use of this resource resulted in increased productivity and therefore larger profits. Benjamin Franklin's dictum – 'time is money' – became a driving philosophy.

The growth and dominance of the capitalist system since the Industrial Revolution has meant that its philosophy of time has continued to dominate western society to the present day. It has seeped into our attitudes and values in various ways – not simply with the idea that 'time is money', but also in our obsession with speed and efficiency, the idea that non-economically productive work like childcare is less valuable than economically productive work, and the idea that laziness is bad and being busy is good. As we've seen, advances in technology and communications during the twentieth and twenty-first centuries have enabled us to achieve ever faster responses to the demands of capitalism, but at the same time have pushed our obsession with speed and efficiency to ever greater heights. We sometimes forget that we have a choice as to the life we want to live, and the speed at which we want to live it.

COMPLEXITY

The world is more complex than ever before. There is more information out there, and more sources of information, than ever before. It is also more difficult than before to identify which elements of this information are useful and relevant to us and which aren't, and what information is reliable and what isn't.

The systems that surround us are also more complex than ever before. For example, in recent years the supply chains, marketplaces and disposal chains for many of the goods and services we consume as individuals have 'gone global'. This has led to the development of a massive and intricate web of complexity behind even the simplest services we use or products we buy. For example, the ingredients of a typical BLT (bacon, lettuce and tomato) sandwich will have travelled over 31,000 miles and been through a huge array of complex processes before the final, simple product reaches the shelves of a supermarket. This increased complexity in the systems around us presents each of us with further challenges. For example, it is difficult to tell who or what we are affecting with each action we take, and in what way we are affecting them.

IDEAS AND INFLUENCES

In the modern world we are surrounded by a varied and complex range of ideas and influences on our thinking. Below are a few examples of some of the most notable areas:

Religion - to a reader in the UK, it may feel as if religion and religious ideas are on the way out, as 52% of UK adults now say they are non-religious. In fact, although religion is on the wane in western Europe and North America, it's growing in most other places. A range of religions are growing, but the largest growth is set to be from Islam, which will overtake Christianity as the world's most popular religion by the middle of this century.[15] Religious ideas influence our lives in a wide range of ways including people's daily lifestyles, their voting habits and the political influence they exert. It's hard to generalise about the influence of religious ideas, but many wars and conflicts are still taking place due to religious tensions, and religious ideas can also tend to promote conservative and traditional values (such as opposing gay

15 www.theguardian.com/news/2018/aug/27/religion-why-is-faith-growing-and-what-happens-next

marriage) and stifle liberalism. On the positive side however they are also responsible for promoting values of compassion and community, fighting inequality and addressing poverty.

Economics - it could be argued that economic ideas are the most influential ones on our lives and societies in the modern world. They not only influence the structures and systems that surround us (for example, those of food supply, welfare and finance), but also carry a number of implicit assumptions and values that filter down into a wide range of areas of our lives, such as how hard we should work and what matters in life.

Throughout the twentieth century, capitalism has been the dominant economic ideology around the world. For the last 40 years or so, western society has been dominated by neoliberalism - a "particularly strong form of capitalism that trusts the financial markets to deliver political, social and other goals and regards state intervention or regulation of any sort as unnecessary and harmful. Under this view, the central aim of a society is to make money, as this is the engine that drives benefits in all other areas."[16] Neoliberalism also carries the belief that constant economic growth is needed.

There are plenty of other economic ideas available with which to govern our world - indeed, there are many shades just of capitalism. It could be argued that this particular brand of capitalism has a very specific view of what matters in human life - for us to be highly productive members of the economy, not only producing economic growth, but also consuming as many goods as possible.

Those of us who live within this system have been brought up with a set of values and ideas that support it - such as the importance of career and material success, the need for hard work and the idea that being busy is a sign that you are somehow worthwhile.

16 Docwra, Richard - Modern Life - as good as it gets?, Green Books, Dartington, 2008, p.89

This economic system is also one of the key drivers behind consumerism and the vast range of influences around us trying to persuade us to buy and consume more stuff, with the (false) promise that this will make us happy.

Politics - there are a wide range of ways in which we could choose to manage our political systems and decide how we should live as groups and societies. These range from democratic systems, in which the people have the authority to choose how they are governed, through to other systems (such as autocratic) in which power rests with a limited number of people, sometimes just one individual. Political systems vary around the world, but below we will discuss the political system that most readers of this book are likely to live within.

Over recent decades in the west our political systems have tended to be democratic, seeking a moderate central ground in politics, whether or not the ruling parties have been left or right wing. In recent years, this has begun to change, with a new dimension of 'internationalism' being added to the old 'left-right' political spectrum of class-based politics, and political views becoming more polarised between different visions. Right wing populism has also been rising in certain countries such as the US - but history shows us that this is unlikely to last forever as political conditions and ideas are continually changing.

One of the ideas that has united people of differing political values for many years, and a key principle behind modern liberal democracies, is that of 'freedom'. This is the idea that each person should be free to live, think and speak as they wish (as long as it doesn't hurt others). There are of course many other ways we could organise politics, but the idea of freedom is such a strongly held principle that we tend to be horrified by ideas or institutions that work against it (such as slavery and authoritarianism), and we use the threat of removing people's freedom (prison) as one of the core punishments in our justice system.

Culture - we each grow up with a range of cultural influences around us that add to the complex mix of ideas in our lives. These cultural influences may come from our family, country, ethnic background, gender and many other areas, which are impossible to summarise here.

THE MODERN WORLD – SUMMARY

In many ways, we are very lucky to be alive at this time. We are living longer than ever before, with better healthcare and education to help us flourish. Yet there are also still many problems, including inequality of not just wealth but of quality of life from childhood upwards (and not just between but within countries), and the damage we are doing to our natural environment (producing global threats like climate change).

We also live in a world with greater complexity than ever before and more messages and influences coming into our brains than ever before - from social media posts to newspaper reports. The modern world also represents a significant challenge for our brains, mental health and ability to carve out independent lives.

We may not realise it but as we grow up each of us is moulded by the ideas and influences that surround us into developing particular attitudes, values and worldviews. And we continue to be influenced like this throughout our lives.

Some of the ideas overarching us in the modern world make these problems more difficult to tackle than they might otherwise be. We need to be aware of the ideas and stories that overarch our society and our individual lives, as well as where they're coming from. We should also challenge them, and remember that these are arbitrary, not actual 'truths', even though they may feel like it sometimes, because they're such a familiar part of our world.

We don't have to follow the ideas or stories that overarch us - we can create our own, better stories. And that is a core part of not just building a better life of your own, but a better society as well. What story do you want to have for yourself and the wider world?

WHAT'S YOUR STORY?

Think about which stories have been most influential in your life so far. The idea that you need to have financial success to be worthwhile? The idea you need to look beautiful? It could be a range of things. List these stories. Now think about whether they are stories that matter to you and that you want to live by. If not, ditch them, and think about what stories (if any) you'd like to live by. Also consider the story you'd like to see the wider world follow. Then savour the sense of release of dropping your old stories and enjoy the new ones!

CONCLUSIONS

In this chapter we have gained some perspective on our lives as human beings living in the modern world. We have stood back and seen where our lives fit into the big picture of the universe and the history of the world. We have explored some of the pressures we currently face and some of the ideas that dominate our thinking and our lives.

So how does this perspective make you feel?

ACTION

HOW DOES THIS PERSPECTIVE MAKE YOU FEEL?

Having read this chapter and seen the context of your life within the bigger picture, how does it make you feel? Reflect on whether it changes your view of life, what you want from it or how you should live.

Hopefully the perspective from this chapter will enable you to look at your life and the world afresh, and help you to challenge a few assumptions you had about your life, society or the wider world.

The next question is what are you going to do with this perspective now? How are you going to apply it so you can live a more considered, fulfilled and compassionate life? Let's move to the next chapter to find out!

CHAPTER 3

WHAT AM I?

What type of creature am I? — What are human beings like? — Is there really a 'me'?

In your life to date, you may not have asked yourself 'What am I?'. This may be because it seems a pointless question - most of us hold it as completely self-evident that we are human beings, that I am 'me' and that the matter needs no further investigation.

But if we dig further into the question of what exactly we are we can gain some very useful self-awareness of how human beings think and behave in particular ways. If we are open-minded enough to accept that we are animals, subject to particular tendencies of thought and behaviour, and can start to understand these tendencies, we can use it to help us lead better informed, more compassionate and more fulfilled lives, as well as build better societies.

In this chapter we will start to build up a picture of the type of creature you are - how you think, how you behave and what your limitations are. We also consider what this thing is that we call 'me' - is there really such a thing as 'me'? This is a less

abstract and far more important question than you might think
- and exploring it can also really enhance our lives!

WHAT TYPE OF CREATURE AM I?

You are a human being - a member of the species homo sapiens.

"Human beings are anatomically similar and related to the great apes (orangutans, gorillas, chimpanzees, and bonobos) but are distinguished by a more highly developed brain and a resultant capacity for articulate speech and abstract reasoning."[17]

Even this short description, and the illustration (above) of human beings standing alongside our ancestors should give us pause for thought. We are animals. Not a supreme, independent being that has simply appeared on this planet out of nowhere but part of a lineage of the great apes that has evolved over millions of years - and that ultimately shares the same single common ancestor as every other piece of life on Earth. And just because we are currently at the far end of the evolutionary line in this picture doesn't mean this is the end of the story - the chances are that other species will evolve from us in the future.

We have explored in earlier chapters how human beings have developed our ideas, knowledge and societies over 200,000

17   www.britannica.com/topic/human-being

years to become the creatures we are now. But 'the creatures we are now' are not that different to the creatures we were 500, 1,000 or 5,000 years ago. We're still subject to many of the same behavioural tendencies, blind spots in thinking and limits to our perspective that we always were. We often don't see this fact though, as it is obscured by the technological developments and complex societies that we've built around us. We think we've overcome ourselves and our nature, but we have not - we are still human beings. So what are human beings like?

WHAT ARE HUMAN BEINGS LIKE?

It is a daunting task to try to characterise human beings as an animal in a general way, in a few sentences. We are complex creatures with complex brains and behaviours, and attempting to make blanket judgements that apply to all 7.7 billion of these creatures is likely to end in a description that's either too general or wildly inaccurate.

So we'll focus on a few common traits that can affect how we think and behave, in order to illustrate how far away we are from the 'rational calculating machines' with complete free will that many of us think we are.

Each of us tends to think that we behave in deliberate, rational ways, our actions driven by conclusions that we've reached for ourselves through rational, calculated thinking. The latest research in psychology, neuroscience and other disciplines is however unearthing a rather different picture - that much of our thinking is instinctive rather than rational, and that we are prone to a range of cognitive biases. Below are a small selection of points from this research just to give some examples of how our assumptions about how we think are wrong.

There is a limit to what we can process at once - our attention is a finite resource - we can only give a limited amount of it at one time. To quote one of the leading experts in cognitive psychology, Daniel Kahneman, "it is the mark of effortful [mental] activities that they interfere with each other, which is why it is difficult or impossible to conduct several at once. You could not compute the product of 17 x 24 while making a left turn into dense traffic, and you certainly should not try. You can do several things at once, but only if they are easy and undemanding."[18]

This finding contradicts many people's beliefs about their own mental capabilities - we all believe we can 'multi-task' - and perhaps we can in very simple activities. But we probably overestimate our capacity for doing this, and could improve our lives (and road safety) by just focussing on one mentally effortful activity at a time - from asking for silence when we are driving through to focussing on one task at a time when we are working.

Value is relative - have you ever found yourself feeling pleased with something you have gained - such as a pay rise - but then noticed your pleasure turning to anger or resentment when you realised that other people had received a better pay rise than you?

If so, it's not surprising, as evidence suggests that our relative status compared to others is a critical factor we use to judge our happiness, rather than what we actually have ourselves. This can be an impediment to our mental well-being, as we may in reality have enough of what we need or want, but feel dissatisfied due to others having more relative to us.

The broader point is that humans do not make judgements in absolute values but rather in relative terms. This applies not just when we compare ourselves to other people, but in most situations - for example, when we have a choice of three price points in buying a product we will tend to choose the middle one, as we are trying to evaluate the costs and benefits of different options so we can arrive at a conclusion as to the value of each.

18   Kahneman, Daniel - Thinking - Fast and Slow, Penguin, London, p.23

This insight on relative value is already being widely applied by influencers the world over. Advertisers try to manipulate us into buying products by asking us to imagine how they will boost our status against other people, and retailers often deliberately add a particularly high priced item in a list of three choices to encourage you to buy the middle priced item (and thus spend more than if you'd been left alone to buy the cheapest one).

Understanding this tendency, and then accounting for it in our thinking, can help us to live more satisfied lives, as well as make us less open to manipulation.

We are programmed to conform - as psychologist Bruce Hood notes, "Our need to conform is a powerful force that shapes us and literally changes the way we think."[19] In other words, there is a physical reaction in regions of the brain when our views differ from those of the consensus.

We are even willing to override the judgements of our senses in order to conform, as was proved by an experiment by psychologist Solomon Asch where he asked people to compare the lengths of different drawn lines and found that people were prepared to give what was obviously the wrong answer in order to conform to the group consensus and avoid being ostracized.

This tendency isn't confined to occasions when we are in the direct presence of a group - it also shapes our behaviour and thinking when away from the group. So, the group has the power to change the views, behaviour and even the perceptions of the individual.

This is borne out by experiments such as the notorious studies conducted by Stanley Milgram at Yale University in the early 1960's, in which ordinary people were prepared to administer a seemingly fatal electric shock to someone, simply because of pressure from an authority figure.[20]

19 Hood, Bruce - The Self Illusion, Constable, London 2012, p.143
20 Hood, Bruce - The Self Illusion, Constable, London 2012, p.146

This propensity for conformity can have some positive implications for our behaviour. For example, it can encourage us to moderate our behaviour when part of a group so that we follow rules and avoid unnecessary conflict. However, it doesn't take much imagination to see the potentially terrible consequences of this tendency towards conformity. It can make people who think of themselves as good behave in bad ways. Even at a less extreme level, it can lead to behaviour and thinking that takes us away from what we would do if we could step back from the situation in which we're being influenced and think about it in a more reflective way.

So, it is good to be aware of this tendency in ourselves and challenge it when it's producing behaviour that conflicts with our considered values and aims.

The effects that this tendency to conform has on our behaviour are more moderate than this most of the time. It is however commonly involved in influencing our behaviour in a range of situations every day in our lives - from making it hard for us to speak up when our views differ from the rest of a group, through to influencing the way some of us dress - following the trends of a group that we are involved in.

We can be good or bad - depending on our environment - following on from the previous point, we would all like to think we are naturally good, and that we are in control of our own behaviour through rational thought, but this does not seem to be the case. Evidence from a range of (often quite shocking) experiments suggests that we are capable of acts of great cruelty if the conditions allow or encourage them.

One infamous example of this is the 1971 Stanford University Prison Experiment in which psychologist Phil Zimbardo simulated a prison setup, using student volunteers in the roles of guards and inmates. Zimbardo found that, by setting up an authoritarian scenario, the students in the guard roles ended up committing acts of cruelty and creating suffering for those in the prisoner roles, even though everyone knew that it was just an experiment and not real.

These experiments show that we are not in control of our behaviour in the way that we think, and that "the situations we can find ourselves in and the influence of those around us determine how we behave and treat others."[21]

These are just a few examples of some of the fascinating insights we are now gaining about how human beings work. We are still relatively early in our knowledge in neuroscience and psychology, but in recent decades we have made profound and important new discoveries that are transforming our understanding of human thinking and behaviour. Many of them overturn some of the common assumptions we've held about our species.

The implications of these insights (and others that have been uncovered by researchers in recent decades) are profound - not just for us but for society at large.

Just as one example, we are more easily influenced by other people than we might think - and this could affect a wide range of ideas and behaviours we have, including the healthiness of our lifestyles, the values we adopt, how we treat other people, whether we decide to speak up against injustice and many other important things.

Another implication of these insights is that human beings are neither intrinsically 'good' or 'bad', but their behaviour can be shaped by a variety of factors - both internal characteristics and external influences. This suggests that we should consider our human tendencies and traits when we develop political policies or review what a 'good society' looks like.

For example, during the coronavirus crisis, governments in Australia and New Zealand recognised that people have the tendency to be too optimistic, so they made their messaging about coronavirus particularly strong. As Daniel Kahneman notes, "Although Humans are not irrational, they often need help to make more accurate judgements and better decisions, and in some cases policies and institutions can provide that help."[22]

---

21 Hood, Bruce - The Self Illusion, Constable, London 2012, p.146
22 Kahneman, Daniel - Thinking - Fast and Slow, Penguin, London, p.411

We should also ensure we build a society in which people's natural traits and 'blind spots' can't be exploited for negative ends by people. This might include banning manipulative advertising, educating children about how we think as human beings and putting more checks and balances in political systems to prevent people's tendency for conformity from being exploited for negative means.

These simple examples alone suggest that it's critical for us, both as individuals and a species to learn this 'species self awareness' - to understand how we think, and apply it to how we live our lives. However, most people have no real conception of how we think and operate as human beings. This stuff isn't prioritised in our education system in any meaningful way.

Also, even within the group of people that do have this conception, many think it doesn't apply to them - that somehow they are a special case because they don't 'feel' these things happening to them - for example, being influenced by group behaviour. A psychology professor reported to me that, having reviewed Milgram's famous experiments outlined earlier with his students, he asked them how they thought they would have reacted in a similar situation. Most of them reported that they would not have administered a shock - which flies in the face of the evidence they had just been taught!

So, a key conclusion here is that it would make our own lives and societies better if we ensured that everyone had a better understanding of our basic traits as human beings, and had the opportunity to consider how we should live our lives and build our societies in the light of this. Perhaps we need to adopt the following principles:

- We should try to live our own lives with greater awareness of the real tendencies and limits to our thinking we have as human beings, as this will help us lead better, kinder and more independent lives.
- We should find ways to educate other people (especially children) about the reality of how we think and behave, for the same reasons as above.

- We need to be much more careful about the values, ideas and culture we are building in society generally, in order to ensure that these encourage prosocial, compassionate and civilised behaviour, rather than the opposite. For example, giving greater status to caring for others than building extreme wealth.

It's important to note that this does not mean that these tendencies and traits are weaknesses of human beings - they are simply how we are. People who describe them as 'weaknesses' - or human beings as 'flawed' - would be failing to acknowledge the creatures that we actually are, and would be comparing us to an idealised and unrealistic vision of humans that doesn't exist but that they've made up in their heads.

ACTION

APPLY YOUR SELF KNOWLEDGE TO YOUR LIFE

Reflect on the points above about our nature and basic traits as human beings. Do they change the way you think about yourself and other people? Reflect, and write a list of ways you could change aspects of the way you think or behave, to improve your life in the light of these insights. If you have time, also consider how society could be improved in the light of them.

IS THERE REALLY A 'ME'?

If you found that the previous section made you reassess who you are, this one may send you over the edge! What if you discovered there was actually no 'you' to start with?

One of the most fascinating topics in psychology, philosophy and neurology is the idea of 'the self' - the centre of the being that I describe as 'me'. Most people would argue that we are more than just our bodies - that there is an individual that occupies my body that I describe as 'me'.

When I wake up in the morning, I have a strong, overwhelming feeling of being 'me'. It is me yawning, and me planning my day or reflecting with anxiety about what someone said about me last night. I feel I am a conscious individual, with my own set of experiences and thoughts.

But psychologists suggest that this idea we have of a solid, consistent self is an illusion - another useful trick that the brain performs in order to help us bring together our experiences and ideas into a meaningful narrative over our lifetime, rather than just having an endless jumble of dissociated thoughts. It is also "faster, more economic and more efficient to treat others as a self rather than as an extended collection of past histories, hidden agendas, unresolved conflicts and ulterior motives. Treating humans as selves optimizes our interactions. We fall in love and hate individuals, not collections."[23]

Imagine instead (correctly) that there is no central thing that is 'you'.

Yes, there is a distinct physical body in which my brain lives that I, and other people, can identify as Richard Docwra. But this does not mean that there is something called 'me' or a central 'self' inhabiting my brain.

It might well feel that there is but that's because our brain is tricking us into thinking this. Instead imagine many layers of memories, feelings, experiences and information that have all built up in your body's brain. The feeling of pain that 'you' experience when hurting yourself in a football tackle. The memory of scoring a goal. The feeling of the pleasant rush of chemicals released in your brain when you win the game. All these layers of information, memories and experience help to give us this false sense of a real, central 'self'.

In other words, "you only exist as a pattern made up of all the other things in your life that shape you. If you take each away, 'you' would eventually cease to exist."[24]

23 Hood, Bruce - The Self Illusion, Constable, London 2012, p.214
24 Hood, Bruce - The Self Illusion, Constable, London 2012, p.215

But this doesn't make our sense of self feel any less real. As Bruce Hood again notes, "the brain hallucinates the experience of 'you' by stimulating its own neural circuits to create that impression. It may be an illusion but it is real as far as the brain is concerned."[25]

Our illusion of having a real 'self' is backed up throughout our lives by the messages we receive from others around us, even though it doesn't really exist. The everyday language we use and the way we relate to each other assumes a self (e.g. 'what are your plans for this evening?') and sometimes these messages are directed at our physical self (e.g. the congratulations 'you' receive when you score a goal) - but all help to support the illusion of a mental 'self'.

There's no problem with the fact that we use this self illusion - it's just one of many ways our brains construct models of the external world in order to help us survive and achieve our goals. But it's fascinating to explore these things and realise that our lives aren't always what they seem! See chapter 4 for some other mind-blowing examples of the ways in which our brains model the world for us.

25   Hood, Bruce - The Self Illusion, Constable, London 2012, p.216

WHY AM I HERE?

What are beliefs? — Why accuracy matters — Is it possible to understand reality? — What should we believe? — Is there a place for religion?

What is the reality we live within? Is the world and universe around us all there is to see? Or are there other dimensions to reality? Is our scientific story of the big bang the whole story - or are we part of a universe made, and watched over, by a higher being?

These questions about reality and belief are some of the biggest questions of life, and we'll explore them in this chapter.

We will start by considering how we can build an understanding of the reality around us, and then consider the benefits of different approaches to doing this - specifically, scientific and non-scientific.

WHAT ARE BELIEFS?

Let us begin by exploring what we mean by the term 'belief'. When we ask this particular question we are attempting to make sense of the world and the reality we find ourselves in.

As human beings, we want to establish reasonable foundations of knowledge on which to build our lives. There is archaeological evidence of religious practices from hundreds of thousands of years ago, which demonstrate that people have been trying to do this long before we were able to write things down (about 5,000 years ago) or before the 'Axial age' (between 900 and 200 BC) when the foundations of many of the world's leading philosophical traditions were established - from the ideas of great Greek philosophers like Plato and Socrates to Confucianism in China.

Early thinkers came up with a range of ideas and explanations for the reality they lived within that can seem quite fanciful to us today. For example, Bronze Age Norse civilisations believed that the sun was drawn through the sky on a chariot pulled by a divine horse.

We should however see these ideas within the context of the time in which they were conceived - times in which people had very few foundations of scientific knowledge to help them understand how the world really worked, but in which people still wanted explanations, stories and ways to control their environment and fates. They came up with ideas that satisfied these needs - just as we would seek to do in their position.

Over the years, our scientific knowledge improved, accelerating over the last few hundred years, and has left us with a firmer set of foundations to help us understand how the world and universe around us works.

Despite the breathtaking array of discoveries we have made about the world and universe in recent centuries, some of the earliest types of belief and ways of seeing the world, such as gods and the supernatural, are still with us. Later in this chapter we will explore why this is the case. As we will see, when we build beliefs about the reality we live in, many people are looking for more than just an explanation of the reality they are living in - they are looking for certainty, comfort, companionship - and more.

WHY IT MATTERS TO HAVE AN ACCURATE VIEW OF REALITY

Let me put my cards on the table at this point. I think it is important for human beings to base their beliefs on an accurate view of reality. Let me summarise why.

There are many reasons why human beings would want to have an accurate view of reality. First, we are curious creatures who want to understand and explore the world around us. We enjoy asking questions and seeking answers.

Second, there are practical reasons why we want to gain control over the world around us. For example - the more we can understand our environment, the better chances we have of surviving in it. Knowing how the seasons work enables us to plant crops at the right time so that we can get a good harvest and feed ourselves. As we have built a more sophisticated understanding of the reality around us, this has also helped us to do things that aren't necessarily critical for our survival but could be seen as strides in our development as a species. For example, we wouldn't have been able to send people to the moon and back or develop the technology for mobile phones if we hadn't made massive strides in very complex physics.

Third, if we don't seek to understand and come to terms with how things actually are, then we put ourselves in danger of being manipulated and exploited. To quote Professor Timothy Snyder of Yale University:

"You submit to tyranny when you renounce the difference between what you want to hear and what is actually the case".[26]

See chapter 7 for some other suggestions on why it is important to be able to think clearly - suggestions which add more ballast to the arguments as to why it matters to have an accurate view of reality.

26 Snyder, Timothy - On Tyranny, The Bodley Head, London 2018, p.66

IS IT POSSIBLE TO UNDERSTAND THE REALITY WE LIVE IN?

Before we consider what the most effective ways are to understand the reality we live in, we should take a step back and ask a more fundamental question - to what extent are we able to understand the reality we live in?

If we are to set realistic expectations for ourselves in this, we need to consider the limitations of the position we're viewing our reality from, the equipment we have to explain it (including our senses, brains, language and mathematics, as well as physical kit like telescopes) as well as the aims we're actually setting ourselves.

WHAT ARE WE ACTUALLY TRYING TO UNDERSTAND?

Let's first try to clarify what we're trying to achieve. By 'understanding reality' most people mean 'have a comprehensive explanation for why we're here and how the universe around us works'.

As we'll see, it's possible to achieve a view of our reality that is quite sophisticated and is more than enough to fill our lives with endless wonder. But it ultimately comes with some caveats, due to the position we are viewing things from - as medium sized creatures with particular senses living in a particular location.

OUR LIMITED PERCEPTION OF REALITY

Before we start to consider the reality around us, we should understand the position we're observing it from. People often fail to do this, and it can make their perception of reality and the world around them very limited and inaccurate.

To illustrate this, imagine if you were looking at the world with blinkers on, and you didn't realise this or reflect on the possibility that it might be the case. You would just assume your restricted view of reality was all there was - and would have no conception of the potential bigger view out there.

By understanding our limited viewpoint, we may still not be able to see as far as we wish, but we will gain a better idea of our limitations and what other views might exist that we are unable to see or conceive of. And this will help us develop a more representative, even if not comprehensive, sense of the reality we exist within.

And, in reality, our viewpoint is limited. We are looking at the world with blinkers on. This is partly due to our limited sensory equipment and processing power as creatures, partly down to our size and partly due to our situation as creatures viewing things from a single viewpoint and location.

Let's start with our senses. If we based our understanding of the world on what our senses told us, we wouldn't realise that radio waves, electricity, or anything else we couldn't see, existed.

We also occupy a particular position in the world and universe, which contributes to our limited perspective and can make it hard for us to see things beyond our current location. For example, from our perspective, as medium-sized creatures living on the surface of the planet, we believed for many centuries (once we had got round to thinking about these things) that the Earth was flat. Similarly, the sun might look like it's revolving, but it's actually us on planet Earth that are spinning. Our experience of things is subjective, but we often forget this. For example, time is relative, but human beings only live for a limited time. If our lives were a great deal longer than they are, we'd see the world quite differently. For example, we'd just see a stone as a temporary coming together of particles of sand.

We should also consider our size and makeup as creatures. In your day to day life you may think your experience of the world is 'all there is' - and is how things really are. It is not. The most fundamental events and interactions in the universe take place at a minute, subatomic level - way smaller than we can see. We only interact with "...a miniscule portion of the innumerable variables of the cosmos."[27] This means we end up only with a blurred view of how things really are. We can only end up with an idea of how the universe is for us.

27   Rovelli, Carlo - The Order of Time, Penguin, London 2018, p.134

As psychologist Daniel Kahneman notes "The world in our heads is not a precise replica of reality."[28] In fact, far from it. We do not see reality as it really is. Our brain constructs models of the external world in order to simplify and translate the data into a form that is useful to help us survive and achieve our goals.

Professor Bruce Hood takes this further: "Our brain simulates the world in order to survive in it...Our brain fills in missing information, interprets noisy signals and has to rely on only a sample of everything that is going on around us. We don't have sufficient information, time or resources to work it all out accurately so we make educated guesses to build our models of reality."[29]

This simulation process involves a lot of shortcuts and rough calculations that can lead to us experiencing the world in ways that are quite unusual and that feel (to us, as the creatures that experience them) more than just the sum of the parts of the chemical, physical or sub-atomic reactions that caused them. Some of these phenomena are central to our experience of life, including our sense of self (discussed in chapter 2), the idea of consciousness and our experience of time.

Let's use the idea of time as an example. The nature of time is a topic that has challenged scientists and philosophers for hundreds of years. As human beings we feel that a real thing called 'time' exists - the past happened, we are now in the present and we look forward to the future. From our perspective, there is a clear, linear passage of time - it moves endlessly forward, and we can never go back.

It turns out that there is no such thing as time that pushes us along in this way. Our particular experience of time is an emergent property of the real physics of time. It is something we experience because of our position and natural makeup as human beings.

When we examine the objective physics of time rather than our experience of it, it turns out that "...there is no single

28 Kahneman, Daniel - Thinking - Fast and Slow, Penguin, London, p.138
29 Hood, Bruce - The Self Illusion, Constable, London 2012, p.xi

time: there is a different duration for every trajectory and time passes at different rhythms according to place and according to speed. It is not directional: the difference between past and future does not exist in the elementary equations of the world:... the substratum that determines the duration of time is not an independent entity, different from the others that make up the world; it is an aspect of a dynamic field. It jumps, fluctuates, materialises only by interacting, and is not to be found beneath a minimum scale."[30]

So, at a very small scale, time doesn't even exist. But, why do we experience the feeling of time passing if it's not really there?

The renowned physicist Carlo Rovelli considers how St. Augustine had a very perceptive view of this, as far back as the 4th Century, and it's based on our experience of music.

"When we listen to a hymn, the meaning of a sound is given by the ones that come before and after it. Music can only occur in time, but if we are always in the present moment, how is it possible to hear it? It is possible, Augustine observes, because our consciousness is based on memory and on anticipation. A hymn, a song, is in some way present in our minds in a unified form, held together by something - by that which we take time to be. And hence this is what time is: it is entirely in the present, in our minds, as memory and as anticipation." [31]

So, to enjoy a tune in the present, we need to remember the preceding notes, hear the current ones and anticipate the next ones. In other words, we're not just thinking of the present, but of the past and future too.

This combination of our memory, plus our continuous process of anticipation of future events therefore leads us to our experience of time.

As Rovelli concludes, "the mystery of time is ultimately, perhaps, more about ourselves than about the cosmos".[32] The same could well be said for many other aspects of reality, including the issue of consciousness. These are profound findings, and it can

30   Rovelli, Carlo - The Order of Time, Penguin, London 2018, p.81
31   Rovelli, Carlo - The Order of Time, Penguin, London 2018, p.157
32   Rovelli, Carlo - The Order of Time, Penguin, London 2018, p.4

give our lives a lot of meaning, fulfilment and clarity to explore them - and the reality of what we see and experience in our lives - further.

In summary then, human beings have quite a restricted perspective and quite a limited experience of reality. Fortunately though, we are curious creatures and have found ways to see beyond this limited perspective. We will explore the most successful of these now.

HOW SCIENCE HELPS US SEE FURTHER

So far in this chapter, we have seen that the 'reality' we experience day to day is an interpretation of reality - a model developed by our brains. It's blurred and simplified in order to make it possible for our brains to process.

The question is, are we able to see beyond this limited vantage point in order to get an accurate picture of reality? Well, to some extent we must be able to see beyond it if we are able to stand back objectively enough to recognise that our experience of reality is just an interpretation of reality.

In fact, we can go a lot further than the restricted, blinkered viewpoint of our everyday experience. To transcend this limited position we need to have the imagination and ideas to come up with explanations for the events around us, and then have the discipline to test these explanations (or hypotheses). This enables us to identify things that we might not be able to find with our senses. And this is, in essence, the scientific method.

As Carlo Rovelli notes, "When we do science, we want to describe the world in the most objective way possible. We try to eliminate distortions and optical illusions deriving from our point of view."

Within the scientific approach we can use objective languages like mathematics to explain the world. To quote another source: "The sciences do not try to explain, they hardly even try to interpret, they mainly make models. By a model is meant a mathematical construct which, with the addition of certain verbal interpretations, describes observed phenomena. The justification

55

of such a mathematical construct is solely and precisely that it is expected to work—that is, correctly to describe phenomena from a reasonably wide area."[33]

Using the scientific method we can make leaps into the unknown, test things and see some of the principles at work. Just go back to our idea of time - which we experience as individuals in a restricted way - and indeed only experience because of our particular makeup as creatures. But we can seek to understand how we come to experience it this way, and seek to get a more objective view of how it works in reality, even if we can't change the way we experience it on a day to day level. And we use the scientific method to do this, by building and testing different models of reality to see which best reflects it. This helps us build a more detailed picture of the universe, and this capacity for learning is one of the great triumphs of human achievement.

This scientific method has helped human beings achieve many things, including greater understanding of, and control over, our external environment, as well as many practical innovations to make our lives easier, healthier and more interesting - from greater yields of agricultural crops to computers and mobile phones.

But are we able to get a completely accurate picture of reality, even with this method? Let us briefly return to our aim in all this. We noted earlier that our aim seems to be to have a comprehensive explanation of why we're here and how the world works. The question is how comprehensive this explanation can be. Are we hoping to explain reality exactly as it is? Or are we happy to just come up with an accurate model that represents reality as we see it?

Ultimately our scientific explanation of reality is also just a model - a representation of it - so we are unable to reach our most ambitious aim of understanding reality as it is. It is the nature of the task that we can't explain the infinite complexity of reality exactly as it is - it just 'is'. But we can develop models

33   Von Neumann, J. (1995), "Method in the physical sciences", in Bródy F., Vámos, T. (editors), The Neumann Compendium, World Scientific, p. 628

to describe it more accurately, and we are constantly striving to build more realistic approximations of the reality we're living in.

The exciting thing is that we are building an increasingly accurate model of how the reality that is accessible to us works, and this will continue to be a source of inspiration, challenge and wonder to us for as long as human beings are around.

ACTION

REFLECT ON YOUR NEW VIEW OF REALITY

Take yourself somewhere quiet and reflect on the new perception of reality you have gained from this section. How does it make you feel about your life, your experience and the world around you?

WHAT SHOULD WE BELIEVE?

So, that's how science helps us understand the reality we exist within, from our starting point as individual creatures with limited perspectives.

Some people don't take this view of the world though, and seek to explain reality in quite different ways, such as the universe being created by a supernatural figure, like a god. Others perhaps follow the scientific view of reality but can't help thinking that there are things we don't yet know that could be supernatural or fantastical, or can't resist believing in fantastical ideas to add colour, comfort and mystery to their existence.

So, what should we believe, and believe in? What is the most effective way for us to try to explain and explore the reality we exist within, from our starting point as individual creatures with limited perspectives? Over the years there have been many ways of doing this, but perhaps two of the most common could be described as the scientific approach and the non-scientific approach. We will briefly explore these now.

This is an emotive question, as it goes deep into the world of people's core beliefs, including religious thinking. The aim of this book is not to be dismissive of religious thinking but to compare it with the scientific method in order to explore the most accurate way of representing reality. We're not going to explore the intentions of religions, but instead, how people interpret and use them. We suggest that some people use and interpret supernatural and religious ideas in an inconsistent, non-critical way - and it's important to adopt a more critical approach to considering what we believe.

People can get very attached to, and emotive about, their beliefs without considering what it is they're trying to explain or achieve with them. If you just believe something 'because you just do' this is not a very useful or convincing reason for why you believe it, as you could believe anything anyone told you. So our aim here is to explore why we might adopt certain viewpoints, and the benefits and drawbacks of adopting each.

It is also important to recognise, as we will explore later, that people don't just adopt their beliefs to be 'correct about the nature of reality' - there are many other reasons, including giving them meaning, wonder, community and stories to live by - but we hope to show simply that a non-religious life can be equally rich, whilst reflecting reality more accurately.

But, back to our core question about reflecting reality.

THE SCIENTIFIC APPROACH

We've established that we live with only a partial, limited view of reality. Assuming that we live in a position of ultimate uncertainty, what's the way of building a realistic view of reality from this position?

One of the good things about the scientific approach is that it enables you to acknowledge and accept these limitations. The fact that there is, and by our nature, will always be, a limit to what we can know. It enables us to be happy with not knowing everything, and to be comfortable with uncertainty and letting doubt in, rather than trying to control it with inaccurate or over-simplified explanations.

Having this sense of humility about our knowledge of reality (or lack of it) can enable us to adopt a perspective about the world that is less dogmatic, better informed and more open to review in the light of evidence. It can also allow us to feel a profound sense of wonder about existence and what's around us, as we journey through the mysteries of life and make discoveries.

Having said all this, we still need to construct a model of reality that is reliable as possible, given our position outlined above.

The scientific approach does this by making a hypothesis (an educated guess) about how a particular aspect of reality works, and then conducting experiments to test whether this hypothesis is accurate - in other words whether it. accurately describes how things work in reality. If the evidence from the experiments show that the hypothesis is accurate, you can 'bank it' as a piece of new knowledge about the world, and then if you want to, undertake more experiments to refine it and learn more or move on to explore another aspect of reality. If the experiments show that the hypothesis is inaccurate however, we can either adjust the hypothesis or abandon it and move on to something else.

This makes the scientific approach rather like a game of snakes and ladders. For every new hypothesis that is proven correct through experiments, we move forward one space. Sometimes we go up a ladder, moving forward several spaces with a fundamental discovery, such as Newton's Mathematical Principles of Natural Philosophy or Einstein's theory of relativity. But much of the time we won't move forward at all as hypotheses are found not to work, and sometimes we might even move backwards, when the results of an experiment show some of the basic assumptions we thought we had proven turn out to not be correct after all.

It is therefore an open-minded process - a willingness to be led not by our feelings, pride or what we want to be true, but by what objectively fits best with reality.

59

Another way of viewing the scientific approach is of beginning a journey into the unknown. We're starting from a position of knowing almost nothing about the reality around us, so we need to find a way of starting to explore and explain this reality, whilst trying to build solid foundations for this knowledge rather than just random guesswork.

To illustrate the benefit of this method, let's consider the approach we'd take to being physically stuck in a position of uncertainty. This is a good analogy as it gives a physical manifestation of the risks we're taking by adopting different views of reality.

Imagine you're trying to move forward from an isolated patch of land in the middle of nowhere. You can't see anything - you have no idea what ground, if anything, lies around you. What would your approach be?

Would it be to:

1. Put a tentative foot out to see what lies outside the patch of land. Cautiously feel for what's around this patch. Then, if your foot landed on something solid, you'd test it to see if it could hold your weight. Then you'd move on to it. And then you'd make a series of tentative, careful steps using the same approach, away from that patch of land.

2. Or would you simply jump off your initial patch of land into the unknown, without any evidence of what's out there or that there are any solid foundations under your feet on your next step?

I suggest the first approach would clearly be the most sensible one, as it's based on testing things out and finding solid ground to stand on before you try to move forward again, rather than risking everything with a random jump into the unknown when you have absolutely no idea whether it's a safe or sensible direction to go in. The first approach can be likened to the scientific approach from our position as human beings in relation to understanding reality. The latter 'random jump' can be likened to the other approach, which we'll explore now.

THE NON-SCIENTIFIC APPROACH

In contrast with the scientific approach, we will now explore just one alternative - what we are calling the 'non-scientific approach'. In essence this is any approach to interpreting reality that doesn't take the disciplined, evidence-led scientific approach, and that instead seeks to put forward an explanation of reality without any proper evidence for it. This could include almost any view not based on evidence - from gods to other supernatural entities or mystical explanations.

These views and beliefs sometimes rely on things other than evidence to give foundations to their views, including the idea of 'faith', which essentially says that the strength of someone's belief in an idea is enough of a foundation for that idea.

As noted in the illustration above, any approach to interpreting reality like this, outside the scientific one of building evidence, does not have strong enough foundations to it - and in fact, has no real foundations, other than the person's own belief in it.

Under this approach to interpreting reality, absolutely any view of reality - however absurd - is equally possible or valid. It is a wild stab in the dark, no better than any other random guess. The view that we are created and overlooked by a god has no more or less evidence than being overlooked by a smurf. You could believe absolutely anything. So, views of reality without foundations to them get us no further at all in understanding reality.

Having read the arguments for the scientific approach though, you may ask 'why should I not believe in a god if I'm just hypothesising this as another step of knowledge - another stepping stone away from our position of ignorance?'.

It's true that we have to use our imaginations and lateral thinking when making any new scientific discoveries and when seeking to take another 'step' of knowledge as discussed earlier. But the 'step' of positing the existence of a god doesn't give us a solid step to move on to, for several reasons:

- It uses some ideas that could be more easily attributed to biases in human thinking (e.g. our image of certain gods being entities that have human figures) than objective attempts to understand reality.
- It's not provable - because there's no evidence for it, and anything that could be offered as evidence for it can be explained by more convincing scientific ideas that can be supported by further evidence.
- It's simply way too big a step to take in knowledge - it is a 'shot in the dark', just as much as it would be if you ignored the scientific approach entirely. This means you might as well posit any belief (eg that the universe was created by smurfs), and it would be as likely (i.e. not very likely) as the god you are positing.

So, whilst we can't prove that god (or any other random supernatural being or far-fetched ideas) doesn't exist, this doesn't mean it's any more likely to exist! And believing so is a mistake of logic - one which many people make.

We could see some of these non-scientific approaches to interpreting reality as perfectly legitimate explanations of the world 2,000 years ago when we didn't have other methods at our disposal of explaining reality or the knowledge and evidence available to support other views. But over the intervening years we've developed these things, and we are now in a position where it looks like a mistake of logic, judgement or reasoning to hold these beliefs as explanations of reality. So, they can be seen as explanations of reality that belong to a bygone, less scientifically sophisticated, age. As we'll see shortly though, people might still hold these views for reasons other than seeking an accurate reflection of reality.

To tie this all up, we suggest it makes sense to live our lives by seeking a view of reality that is as accurate as possible. To do this, we should adopt the scientific approach, which builds a model of reality in a cautious, objective and logical way.

Contrary to what you might think, this doesn't lead to a bland, technical view of the world and nor does it eliminate the need for imagination on our part. We simply don't need additional mystery to our existence in the form of undiscovered supernatural entities - as the reality of our existence is already utterly mind-blowing (read the earlier section about time again!) and will yield many more breathtaking and imagination-defying discoveries as we go along. And to make these discoveries we still need amazing leaps of imagination and thinking by human beings.

As you'll see throughout this book, the scientific approach can help us come up with a clearer perspective on the world on a range of questions, including the meaning of life (see the next chapter for details), the reality we live in (as we've explored here) and how to live and die well (see chapter 11).

WHY THE MOST ACCURATE IDEAS AREN'T ALWAYS THE MOST POPULAR ONES

If the scientific approach is the most accurate way of representing reality we might ask why many people still harbour non-scientific beliefs, and why religious ideas, although on the decline in the UK, are actually growing in popularity around the world.

The answer could be a combination of factors, including people's motivations for adopting particular beliefs (which we will explore in the next section 'Is there a place for religion?') and some basic tendencies in human thinking and behaviour. We will explore the latter point now.

People don't believe ideas just because they're true - it's not the realism or accuracy of ideas that makes them influential or believed by people. It's more complicated than that for humans. As we've seen earlier in this book, we have a range of traits and tendencies in our thinking and behaviour (such as the tendency to conform) that mean we are not 'rational calculating machines' that simply identify the most accurate or logical answer to a question and choose that. We are vulnerable to influence and to ideas that aren't true.

Ideas can therefore 'stick' with individuals and groups of people even if they are inaccurate, but are supported by tradition ('this is what we've always believed'), authority ('this is what you must believe') or other influences. Many of the views that human beings have had about reality - and other things - have spread because of power and other influences, rather than their veracity. For example, the Christian view of the world became popular not because it was the 'right' one but because the Roman empire indoctrinated people with it around the continent as it expanded.

As a parallel, we can see a reduction in trust in science and an increase in anti-scientific ideas (like the movement against vaccinations) in countries like the USA where leaders and national media promote such ideas and enable them to flourish. Ideas - whether good or bad ones - just need the right conditions to thrive, and they will do so, regardless of their veracity.

It can also be seen how ideas that have been accurate have been actively suppressed by people in power who don't like their ideas being threatened - for example, in 1633 astronomer Galileo Galilei correctly claimed that the Earth orbited the Sun, yet was found guilty of heresy against the Catholic

Church for this claim, as it contradicted the Church's view that the Sun orbited the Earth. His publication was banned and he was placed under house arrest for the rest of his life. The Church only accepted his views 300 years later!

When you consider your beliefs and views about reality or any other issue, you therefore need to challenge any that appeal to authority, tradition, popularity or anything other than the veracity of their view to justify them, and instead judge them on their own merits, finding out for yourself what the real evidence for them is. We should also take care to ensure that we represent our views in this way when discussing them with other people, and fight for a political system that promotes knowledge, evidence and learning rather than a 'free for all' approach to beliefs and ideas.

Some beliefs can be very 'sticky' - they can become embedded in our lives. They can be at the centre of how we identify ourselves, and once we identify ourselves as being of a particular religious denomination, it can be hard (and sometimes extremely painful, emotionally and psychologically) to move away from this. A similar argument can be made for certain types of political ideology, which can also be particularly powerful, 'sticky' influences on people.

Some belief systems can also be 'closed systems', which have a range of functions within them to stop people from moving away from them – including claiming that they worship the one 'true' god, that other religions are wrong and that apostates will receive punishment in this life or after death if they leave the religion.

We're good at rationalising our beliefs - another factor that can prevent us from arriving at the most reasonable view of something is the fact that human beings are good at rationalising the things we already believe rather than altering our position and changing our beliefs. For example, we can rationalise evidence that does not support our existing beliefs to make it fit with them, or can selectively choose bits of evidence that support our existing beliefs and prioritise these, whilst ignoring the greater weight of evidence against our beliefs.

The solution here seems to be for us to go through a similar process to the scientific approach when deciding what to believe about the world. We can build our beliefs, but should be willing to drop or adapt them in the face of better evidence. We will need to be brutally honest with ourselves when we do this, and this can require greater courage that we might expect, as it can mean being willing to challenge the ideas we hold dear, as well as the worldviews that shape our lives.

To assist ourselves in doing this, perhaps we should even consider not getting so attached to our beliefs, and not letting them define us in the way that we sometimes do. This would make it easier for us to drop or adapt them in the face of better evidence rather than feeling we are 'losing face' or being personally attacked or undermined when our views and beliefs are challenged.

IS THERE A PLACE FOR RELIGION?

We have now considered different ways of formulating our beliefs about reality, as well as some of the ways we might unwittingly be moved to adopt beliefs that are less accurate reflections of reality.

Some non-religious people may be inclined to mock people with religious or supernatural views for believing things that are far-fetched and without evidence. But some religiously-minded people would argue that they gain a rich range of benefits from their beliefs that can't be provided by a scientific view of the world. And that they specifically adopt these non-scientific beliefs for this very reason - choosing a belief system that will give them a richer, more comforting life, rather than a more accurate view of the world.

In this final section of the chapter we will explore some of the reasons why some people might actively choose to adopt a non-scientific approach to belief, and consider whether these benefits can only be gained through these types of belief, or whether they can also be derived by someone who adopts a scientific approach to understanding the world.

WONDER, MYSTERY AND IMAGINATION

Some proponents of non-scientific beliefs would suggest that these outlooks have a greater sense of wonder, mystery and colour than a purely naturalistic worldview, which can be rather grey and mechanistic - but this is far from the case.

There is a view that non-scientific explanations give us an escape from our rational daily lives lived 'within the normal world', and the thrilling idea that there is 'something more out there' beyond that which we know and see.

This might be in part a yearning for wonder and mystery - almost a desire to feel like we did when we were children about the magical world out there that we had not yet discovered or understood, but which turned out to be more mundane than we thought when we became adults.

There are several responses to this thinking. The first is that the world isn't mundane. The scientific model of reality provides a multitude of wonders. In fact, as we've seen, its whole aim is to take us outside the limitations of our perspective as individual humans. And when we do this we get a completely new perspective on reality that transcends our personal experience of life, and can fill us with wonder (just return to our discussion of 'time' earlier for an example of this). So, there is much wonder and escape to be had in a scientific view of the world.

A further response is that this feeling of 'knowing all there is to know about the world' is, in most people, completely misplaced. People don't generally understand the world half as well as they think when they are adults! Most people are completely unaware of the wonders of the reality we live within, and if they were they might gain the 'escape from the mundanity of day to day life' that they wanted.

We should also try to unpick the Idea that there are fantastical things out there waiting to be known that we don't know. Well, there are - but they may just not be in the pre-judged or pre-anticipated form that people imagine - and we need to be open to that. So, contrary to how the argument often runs, the scientific worldview is actually more open minded and open to bizarre discoveries than other views, which can have pre-supposed conceptions of what these 'mysteries' might look like, such as gods or auras - which doesn't make them a mystery, just a belief in something specific but random!

A final observation is that some people just don't want to always be living in reality - they want a break from it. And who can blame them? Perhaps one of the most convincing strategies for tackling life is to adopt the scientific approach to reality, but deliberately take breaks from reality sometimes when we need to. And this is the route that many people take, using a variety of means to do it, including fantasy, imagination, novels, science fiction and, with far greater risks to their health, drugs.

It can be strongly argued then that it's possible to live lives containing just as much wonder, mystery and imagination in a non-religious way as in a religious way. The non-religious approach means that the individual just has a more accurate view of reality in the background, and remains grounded to this even when they take their breaks from reality.

BETTER VALUES

A claim that is sometimes made for religious thinking is that it provides more reasons for people to behave in a good way than non-religious thinking - including the threat of punishment by a deity. But, as we will see when we get to the values section, you don't need to be religious to be moral, and in fact it can sometimes obscure our moral compass to be religious. But that's for another chapter.

RITUAL

Although ritual can be seen to be an important and profound part of many spiritual practices, its use clearly does not have to be confined to the religious world.

STORIES

Some people with religious views would argue that religious ideas are not specifically about reality - they aim to tell stories to inspire people, build wisdom and show them how to lead good lives. And this is of course a worthy aim.

But even if this is the core purpose of religious ideas, there are plenty of other stories we could draw upon for this purpose - from great literature to other ideas. Rather than attach oneself to a religion, it would seem to make more sense to draw upon stories from a wide range of sources - both religious and non-religious (including works of great literature) to inspire and advise us in life.

We can do this whilst retaining the more accurate beliefs about reality brought by the scientific worldview, and the wisdom, values and perspective brought about by a thoughtful and well-informed approach to living, without needing religious ideas.

NOT FEELING ALONE

Over the centuries, religion has played another role that is important for many people - providing a sense that they are not alone.

This is not just in terms of providing them with social support and company in their daily life, but also at a much broader and more profound scale - giving them a sense that they are not alone in their existence in the universe. It could be seen as 'a solution to eternal aloneness'.

This is a particularly interesting issue, as one might well ask why people need to not feel alone. After all, many of us are surrounded by other people from the moment we are born to the moment we die, and within our lives we can - to a certain extent - choose how much time we spend with other people.This doesn't feel like overwhelming isolation. So why do we need to feel less alone?

Perhaps it is partly driven by a fear of death (which we will come to in the next point) and also by the human need for companionship. It could also be due to a fear of the unknown. If people are not willing or able to face the realities of our existence that we've outlined in this book, or the fact that there is a lot that we just don't know about our existence and the reality around us, then they may prefer to resort to imagining things. But, as we aim to show below, we don't need to do this.

First let's look at religion's role in bringing people together. Its force as a way of binding people together is unquestionable, and one of the biggest benefits of being part of a religion is to feel part of a wider community, share a common sense of identity and have regular opportunities for communal and social activities.

We don't need religion to achieve a similar sense of shared humanity though, and with a non-religious viewpoint we can extend this feeling to all humans, not just those our religion tells us to or who share our views and beliefs. Using our sense of perspective, we can feel empathy and love not just for human beings but for all the other creatures we share this planet with.

We can also find practical ways of increasing our sense of connection with others on a day-to-day basis. There are fewer formal structures to bring us together than in the religious world of churches and regular congregations, but we can get involved in various ways with our neighbours, communities and other groups (from sports to social clubs) that can give us a real sense of connection to others. Helping other people is one of the most powerful and rewarding ways of building these connections.

And now to the broader question of 'existential aloneness'. One need that seems particularly important to some is the desire to feel connected to someone else at all times - that they are not on their own. This need for an ongoing relationship may stem from the feeling of having a parent's care and support watching over us in childhood, but could also be a simple human need for contact.

Some people may need to believe in this ongoing relationship so much that they will conjure one up even when they know it's not 'true'. So the idea of a relationship with someone (such as a supernatural power or imaginary friend that will never leave us and never die is incredibly attractive and strong.

Perhaps some people see life as a fight against isolation, and death as the ultimate isolation. Religion is the cure for being alone - both in this life and forever - with an all-good figure who'll never let you down.

So, what is the naturalistic, non-religious response to this question of existential isolation? The main response is that the question itself is irrelevant.

First, we could observe that we're rarely alone in our lives. At the start of life, we are carried within another person for nine months and then delivered into the arms of one or more people who will (generally) look after us carefully for years after this point. Up to the point of death, some of us die alone, but many people die around people who are caring for them and wishing the best for them.

In between these points we have many opportunities to connect with other people as we go through our lives. Even at times where we are feeling alone and isolated, we can either enjoy this solitude or console ourselves with the connections we do have in the real world - even if they aren't with us at the time. Loneliness can be excruciating - but the idea of an imaginary friend or parent watching over us is ultimately just a mental illusion we are building for ourselves, and if we wanted, we could build this temporarily without having to subscribe to further fantastical belief systems as part of it.

Before birth and after the point of death, we have no need for company as we simply don't exist. And perhaps this point is the most difficult thing for people to face - the idea of not existing.

It can be hard to get our heads around the idea of not being alive when we are alive, and many people fear (or simply can't comprehend) the idea of 'nothing'. We must do so though if we

71

are to live with a reasonably accurate sense of reality - and in this book we aim to offer a different, better-informed way of looking at life and death that can help us overcome our fear and incomprehension of death and 'nothing'.

As we have tried to argue in this book, we should see life as the exception rather than the norm - a brief moment of existing in an otherwise featureless landscape of non-existing - and therefore that it's existing that's the unusual thing, not not-existing!

So, perhaps the issue we are discussing in this section is the fear of not existing as much as being alone. But in either case, a non-religious person might argue that we need to face up to these things as simple facts of reality - not things we should be seeking to avoid by building fantastical belief systems around them. Ultimately you are no less alone with the non-scientific worldview than with the scientific one.

With a scientific worldview we can also find a completely different way of framing our existence and relationship with others. For example, given our modern understanding of physics at a very small scale, we can show that you and everything else in the universe are just a collection of particles that briefly coalesce as particular objects (like 'you'), but are moving around all the time. So you are simply part of the universe, made up of the same building blocks as everything and everyone else. You, other people and the universe are one and the same thing - which is quite a comforting thought!

FEAR

We have explored a couple of specific fears that religious and supernatural ideas might help us to ignore or feel better about, but it could be argued that these types of thinking can give people answers and comfort to things they're more generally scared or uncertain about.

People have always looked to gods and the supernatural to control and explain things when they can't control or explain them themselves. Just recall how people have offered prayers and ceremonies to gods at harvest time when they are desperate for a good crop.

This approach may have been all we had several millennia ago, but we now have a (scientific) method to help us build our understanding of the world around us and increase our level of control of our external environment. But, as our current level of knowledge shows us, there are still many things we don't know, and plenty of things we can't control.

So, the question seems to be about how we should react in a situation of doubt and uncertainty. Over the years, religious views have acted as a balm for us - finding a broad way to explain everything and giving us a sense of agency in the universe. But these explanations are very simplistic and don't stand up to much scrutiny in the modern age.

The scientific approach says that we have to be prepared to accept doubt and uncertainty as part of our lives given the position we are in as creatures. We don't have to build random fantasies around us to escape from the fears that we've conjured up for ourselves due to our fear of the unknown or desire to have a neat explanation for everything. Instead we can come to an accommodation with these things, whilst still being driven by our curiosity to better understand the reality we live in.

This approach also tells us that there's no reason why we should expect to be in control of our external environment, but we can also become better at controlling it through building our knowledge, and this also helps us identify the things that we can't control, as well as to accept this fact.

As a final point, religious ideas can act as a salve to people's general anxieties in life, beyond fear of death and the unknown, and can provide a sense of comfort - a feeling that there is 'something more' beyond the suffering they are experiencing in this world.

This is quite an understandable response from someone who is suffering in life - for example through extreme poverty or illness. Our answer to this, as people with moral values, should be to try to reduce this suffering and build a society where suffering like this is minimised.

But everyone is likely to experience suffering at various points in their lives, and even if someone is suffering, this doesn't change the reality they are actually living in.

Overall it is up to us as individuals whether we want to hide from life's realities with stories and fantasy, or whether we want to live with an honest and realistic view of reality. In this book we have suggested that taking the latter approach brings a number of major benefits. We can add to this that it also brings a sense of dignity - to be a human being that has used their intellectual skills to live with an accurate sense of reality and has had the courage to face this reality.

SUMMARY

Overall we're conflicted creatures. We're curious and want to understand things 'as they are', but at the same time we also want comfort and fantasy, and want to feel that everything will be OK. This is why many people end up with inconsistent, muddled views of the world. But it doesn't really feel consistent to have both - you need to either accept things as they are or live within a life of stories. But accepting things as they are doesn't mean losing the opportunity for wonder and meaning - it's there all around us and in our heads.

In conclusion then, it is your choice on the beliefs you adopt. But we suggest that, if you want to live with a view of reality that is as accurate as possible, the scientific approach is the one to adopt.

As we've seen though, this is not just about our beliefs in the reality we live in. As Alain de Botton writes: "God may be dead, but the urgent issues which impelled us to make him up still stir and demand resolutions which do not go away when we have been nudged to perceive some scientific inaccuracies in the tale of the seven loaves and fishes."[34]

You might therefore choose to adopt the scientific view of reality whilst taking some religious or other views because you feel they bring greater richness and comfort to your life than

34   De Botton, Alain - Religion for Atheists, Penguin, London 2013, p.12

a purely naturalistic worldview. And again, this is your choice. But, as we've explored in the latter part of this chapter, we suggest that some of these supposed benefits of a non-naturalistic worldview aren't benefits at all, but refusals to face reality, and that others are provided equally well by the scientific worldview, in addition to it providing a conception of life and existence that is positive, wondrous, and in its own way, comforting. And that is what this book overall is trying to set out.

As noted earlier in this chapter, we can only explore these viewpoints briefly as we have limited space, so we are not trying to demean the great richness and fulfilment that people gain from religious and other forms of beliefs and experiences, and the reader can explore these areas in greater detail at their leisure. We are simply making the argument that there is an equal, if not greater, level of richness, joy and wonder to be gained in a life that is not tethered to such beliefs. And this view also yields a more accurate view of reality.

ACTION

REFLECT ON WHAT YOU BELIEVE

When you've read this chapter, reflect on your view of reality. What approach do you want to adopt to interpreting the reality you live in? Why do you want to adopt this approach? Then consider how adopting this approach might influence your view of life and how you should see it and live it.

PART 2

TOOLS FOR THE JOURNEY

CHAPTER 5

HOW CAN I EXPLORE THE EXPERIENCE OF BEING ALIVE?

What is life? - What does it mean to be alive? — Is life really a journey? — How can we explore our inner lives? — What does it feel like to be alive? — Peak experiences - Mindfulness — Exploring your thoughts

We know that human beings are living creatures. But what does it mean to be alive as a human being? And what does it actually feel like to be alive?

These are profound questions, and exploring them can help us lead richer and more fulfilled lives. We will look at them in this chapter, as well as the broader topic of how to explore our inner lives.

WHAT IS LIFE?

This may not be a question that you have asked yourself very much because it's something we take for granted. But if we probe it a little deeper, we can develop a better perspective on our lives and how to live them.

We gave a scientific definition of life in chapter 3. But this was an external, unattached view. What is life from the point of view of someone actually living right now?

One thing to mention at the start is that I can only really say what it means to be alive for me - from my subjective perspective. It's a reasonably well-known philosophical argument that we can only know what's going on inside our own heads, and can never truly know what it's like to be someone else. A classic explanation of this is in philosopher Thomas Nagel's brilliantly-titled short essay 'What is it like to be a bat?'. So, all we can do is take our own personal experience and assume that other people share a similar one, based on the things we tell each other through our written, verbal and other communications with each other.

We also have to assume that other animals may have a different experience of life - and probably one that is less reflective about it too. So, the experience of life that we discuss in this chapter is limited to a human perspective.

But perhaps we can define life as follows - as the period of 80 years or so[35] in which we find ourselves conscious and sentient.

This is a reasonable summary of what life is - from the perspective of someone living it. But there is another way in which we can look at, and define life - and that's to describe it in relation to the content of our experience when we're going through this period of consciousness and sentience.

From a subjective point of view, being alive is perhaps the experience of being 'switched on' as a creature. Both before our brain reaches a certain developmental point when we are in the

---

35 This is an average lifespan. Some people will of course live longer than this, and some will sadly live much shorter lives. But throughout this book, we will refer to this roughly 80 year period, as it helps to focus our minds on the finitude of life.

womb, and from the moment we die, we have no experience at all - we are essentially switched off. Either way, it seems that our experience within this limited period of time is all there is for us as subjective, experiencing individuals.

This has some profound consequences for how we should think about and live our lives, as well as how we should think about death. We'll explore these in more detail in the final chapter of this book, 'How to deal with death and getting older'.

WHAT DOES IT MEAN TO BE ALIVE?

We could see our period of existence in a number of ways. For example being alive is:

• Something we didn't ask for and had no choice in. Therefore, we could feel annoyance about about being alive.
• A fight for continued survival.
• A big risk - in which something bad could happen to us at some point.
• A remarkable opportunity to exist.

There are lots of other ways you could interpret life, and these are just examples. It seems reasonable though to say we don't have any choice in being born, and that you only get to be alive once as the specific 'self' you are today. The way we interpret life could therefore be anything from seeing life as an amazing opportunity to enjoy or something harsh or fearful to endure.

We can adopt any of these, or limitless other, views we like. And our view on this may affect how we choose to live our lives and what meaning we derive from them. For example, a positive view of life as an opportunity to exist may make someone live anything from a considered, reflective life savouring every moment to a hedonistic life looking to gain as much pleasure as possible, where they are more concerned with quality of life than length of life. A negative view of life may lead people into a risk-averse way of living in order to avoid harm as much as possible, or again a more hedonistic one where they don't really care what happens to them. A wide range of possibilities for life flow from both the positive and negative views.

It is interesting to reflect on whether each of us subconsciously carries any of these assumptions about life with us, and whether they are reasonable or helpful in our lives - as if they're not, perhaps challenging them could help us live happier, more fulfilled lives. This is because our interpretation of life - and the conclusions about how to live that we derive from it - could be something that we could change.

ACTION

HOW DO YOU SEE LIFE?

Have a think about the assumptions you carry with you about life. This may take a little time to reflect on, as we don't often think about this, but try to think about some of the subconscious assumptions you make about life or how things will turn out. Then consider whether they are helpful in your life - and if not, whether adopting a different interpretation of life and set of conclusions on how to live, could make life better. If so, note them and try to adopt them. Return to your list when you feel a need to remind yourself of this more helpful interpretation of life.

We explore the question of the meaning and interpretation we all give to life in more detail in chapter 6 - 'How can I find meaning in my life?'.

IS LIFE REALLY A JOURNEY?

There are many ways of describing life in relation to the content of our experience. One of the most common is to characterise it in a linear way - as a type of a progression or a journey. After all, it has a clear starting point and a brutally clear end point - along with plenty of twists and turns in between.

But one danger of describing life as a journey is that this particular journey can be cut short at any point, without you reaching the destination you had intended.

We don't have to look at life in this linear way though. We can come up with any metaphor or model that we like to interpret it. For example, we could see it as a brief spark of existence in an otherwise eternal void of non-existence. Or we could view it without the idea of 'time' at all - and instead see it as a range of different states, sensations, feelings and events that occur in and around us.

And perhaps the way we choose to characterise life actually influences how we experience it. For example, if we see life as a journey, then might we not in old age be tempted to feel that we're somehow 'winding down' or reaching the end of our journey - and might this compel us to slow down and essentially write life off in later years? Hopefully people don't do this, but it's easy to see why they might if they followed this interpretation of life.

ACTION

THINK ABOUT HOW *YOU'D* CHARACTERISE LIFE

Have a think about different ways to characterise life, and how each might influence you to think or live differently. We don't have to choose a specific one to adopt - but perhaps there are some useful insights and perspectives to take from each one?

Perhaps the idea of the journey is the best model we have for life, but we should realise that it's an arbitrary, made up view and should take care not to assume that there is a particular destination we are going to reach - as we may not reach it. It may be better, as many novelty tea towels will tell you, to simply 'enjoy the journey' rather than seek a particular destination, or assume you are going to reach it. This could help us appreciate life more, not take it so seriously, and get the most out of it - no matter what stage in the journey we're at.

HOW CAN WE EXPLORE OUR INNER LIVES?

So far in this chapter we have touched a couple of topics that have helped us to start exploring our inner lives. Let's explore this a bit more now.

Spirituality, the big questions, our inner lives, consciousness – call it what you like, but human beings have explored this issue for thousands of years, and doing so can nourish and enhance your life, regardless of whether you hold religious views or are a committed atheist.

Another way of looking at this is exploring the world in your head. There's a world 'out there' full of people, trees, televisions and other things, but when we close our eyes and shut ourselves off to this there is also a 'world in your head' which is just yours.

This includes some of the big questions of life that we discuss elsewhere in this book such as your beliefs (see chapter 4), the self (chapter 3) and how to manage your thoughts (chapter 7), but also includes a number of other important areas such as your imagination, peak experiences and overall what the author Christopher Hitchens called 'the numinous and transcendent'. We will explore some of these further areas in the remainder of this chapter.

From a scientific perspective these thoughts, experiences and worldviews in our heads are simply physical phenomena - electrical impulses and chemical reactions - but for us as the creatures living with them, they form a large part of our experience of life and bring much of the richness of this experience. So there is clearly value in exploring them, whatever their origin may be, if we are to make the most of our few decades experiencing life.

For centuries, religions have provided many people with the chance to tackle these questions, but as the West has become less religious, very few institutions have moved into this space to help people explore their inner lives. This has left a big gap in many people's lives, and we need new institutions and a new way of talking about our inner lives that is open to everyone, including the non-religious.

Most of us explore our inner lives at some point - whether we realise it or not. We're inquisitive creatures and even those people who see themselves as resolutely unreflective will probably have spent some time considering why they are alive or what it's like inside their head.

Ultimately, exploring the world in our heads is just part of what it means to be human. As far as we know we are the only animals on the planet capable of this type of reflective, abstract thought. It therefore seems to make sense that most of us would make use of this capacity at some point in our lives. It doesn't follow that we should do this - but if we have a capability it is likely we would try to exercise it at some point.

WHAT DOES IT FEEL LIKE TO BE ALIVE?

Another way to phrase this question is 'what does it feel like to be conscious'?

At this point it is extremely tempting to embark on a discussion on the issue of consciousness.

We won't be doing this here, even though it is fascinating and remains one of the great mysteries of our time. We have put some references at the end of this chapter for you to explore it further if you'd like to.

We will instead focus our attention less on the academic and philosophical idea of consciousness and more on what it actually feels like for us to be conscious.

How can we describe the feeling of being alive? Perhaps there are two main areas that contribute to our feeling of being alive:

Senses - first, most of our experience of the external world is gained through our senses, including sight, hearing, smell, touch and taste. There are other senses beyond these 5 main areas, including proprioception - the sense of where your body and limbs are in space.

Our minds and thoughts (conscious and unconscious) - even without sensory data, our minds can help us explore and make sense of the reality that we're experiencing and living in, as well as provide us with content that affects our experience of life - for example, in the form of our thoughts and emotions.

So what does it feel like to be a living creature stuck within your mind and body?

This is again a subjective experience, so before we attempt to articulate our experience here, try it for yourself. Here's how.

One of the great pleasures of life is to ignore all the thoughts rushing through our heads and the day-to-day concerns that take up much of our attention, and simply identify and appreciate the experience of being alive. This is similar to the experience of meditation, but the exercise we suggest trying below is more about sitting quietly and identifying what it feels like to be alive - what your senses and experience feels like - and then savour this very special state.

You can reflect on your experience in any context and setting - not just in a place that is still and peaceful. For example, you can reflect on your response to the different stimuli around you (such as art, music and literature), noticing how these affect you and how you interpret them. If we have the strength and presence of mind to do so, it can also be valuable to reflect on our experience of other sensations and emotions such as pain and joy. Doing so can not only help us learn about ourselves but also give us comfort during difficult times.

JUST BE

Find a quiet place to sit, and ignore the thoughts rushing by in your head. Focus on what it feels like to be alive at this moment. What you're experiencing through your senses. Notice your feelings. Observe how this is all coming together in a central experience of being 'you', alive right now. And savour this experience.

My personal experience of this process is a peculiar feeling of being 'switched on' - being a creature that is buzzing with life, even in the fuzzy colours I see through my eyelids while my eyes are closed. I have a sense of having the potential for movement or action at any time, thanks to the latent physical energy in me.

When I actually think about what it feels like to be alive it can feel quite overwhelming. A deluge of senses and thoughts working at the same time, even when one is sat quietly. It's as if I am the central processing hub of lots of sensory data and thoughts, all passing through me at the same time, and this is happening constantly throughout my life.

To feel like this about life every living moment would be quite exhausting, so it's fortunate that, as human beings, we seem able to ignore the overwhelming nature of this in our day to day life and just focus our attention on specific things, such as the fact that we're hungry or that we need to catch the next train in 10 minutes.

But it can certainly add to the clarity of our perspective on life, as well as increase our sense of fulfilment (both of which we're trying to do in this book) to take time to reflect on this properly. If we can identify, reflect on and truly feel the mental and physical processes we are going through when we are alive, this reveals some important truths to us about our humanity and status as living creatures.

HOW CAN WE FIND PEAK EXPERIENCES?

Peak experiences are those rare and wonderful times in which we feel a profound sense of peace, pleasure, immersion in an activity, connection with the world and contentment with our place in the great scheme of things. Moments where we get goosebumps.

Charles Darwin described one such moment when he was exploring South America - feelings that you may recognise when you've been in a beautiful natural setting:

> *"In my journal I wrote that whilst standing in the midst of the grandeur of a Brazilian forest, 'it is not possible to give an adequate idea of the higher feelings of wonder, admiration and devotion which fill and elevate the mind'."* [36]

Darwin seems to be describing the experience of realising he is a very small part of a vastly bigger thing (the universe and the natural world), as well feeling a sense of connection with this broader universe. Not only this but he is appreciating the beauty and size of the forest - and the natural world in general - surrounding him.

These experiences can occur during a range of activities and situations, and may differ for each of us. These peak experiences can be beneficial for us in a number of ways, and not least because they are some of the moments that make life worthwhile.

The founder of much of the modern scientific exploration of peak experiences was the psychologist Abraham Maslow. He described some of the characteristics of peak experiences as follows:

- **Awesome** – there is a sense of awe, wonder and humility within the experience.
- **Timeless** – the person having the experience can lose track of time, and become oblivious of his or her surroundings.

36 Darwin, Charles - The Life and letters of Charles Darwin Vol 1, Adamant Media, London 2001, p.134

- **Rich** – the perception of the object in the experience (if there is one - such as a picture, piece of music or view) can be richer in a peak experience.
- **Egoless** – you may be so focussed on the experience that you lose track of your worries, fears and concerns, and you lose your sense of 'self' during the experience.
- **Valuable in itself** – many of the things we do in life are means to some other end – for example, getting a job so that we can earn money to buy food to help us survive. Some peak experiences however can be seen as 'ends in themselves' – we do them because they are valuable in themselves and can even be said to make life worthwhile by their occasional occurrence.
- **Perspective** – the experience generates a type of perspective – the person is able to "perceive the world as if it were independent not only of them but also of human beings in general". In other words, they are able to see the world from a position beyond simply human interests.
- **Complete** - the object or the experience is felt to be all there is in the universe – to be synonymous with the universe itself.

Another characteristic we could add to this list is that many peak experiences are immersive - the person is completely absorbed and immersed in the experience. For example, getting lost in a piece of beautiful music.

You may be able to recall some experiences in your own life that have included some of these characteristics. We can gain peak experiences through a wide range of places, activities and contexts, and these will differ for everyone. The important point is that everyone can find them in their lives.

Below are a few examples of activities or situations in which people have reported having peak experiences:

- **Nature** - many people (including the author) have had peak experiences when out in the countryside and absorbed in the natural world. Jonathan Haidt, in his interesting book 'The Happiness Hypothesis', notes one explanation for this:

"Something about the vastness and beauty of nature makes the self feel small and insignificant, and anything that shrinks the self creates an opportunity for spiritual experience." [37]

- **Immersive activity** - some activities are automatically immersive, requiring concentration to undertake them successfully or remain safe doing them – for example, doing a crossword, singing, playing the piano, riding a motorbike or playing a sport. Activities that require practice and effort to be able to learn the skills to do them can provide an additional sense of fulfilment and pleasure when carrying them out.
- **Creativity and inspiration** - creative acts such as painting, writing, creating a song or cooking can also be immersive and have the potential for producing peak experiences. Another area that is thought to regularly yield peak experiences is scientific achievement – making a discovery or solving a complex problem after a long period of time. Very few people are great scientists, but the general areas of problem solving and generating ideas could be possible sources of peak experiences for many people.
- **Arts** - another area in which people have reported peak experiences is in appreciating art. This can be art in any form, including viewing a great picture, listening to a piece of music that moves you or hearing beautiful singing.
- **Meditation and relaxation** - this includes a general set of activities in which the participant is encouraged to relax in peace and calm their mind. These are activities in which one is encouraged to slow the river of one's thoughts and just 'be' without thinking of anything. They could include yoga, reflection and meditation – the latter being an activity that some people undertake specifically to reach a state of peak experience, or something similar to it.

37   Haidt, Jonathan - The Happiness Hypothesis, Arrow, London 2007, p.200

These are just a few illustrative examples of situations or activities in which people might have peak experiences. There are many other areas we've missed out, including listening to a great speaker, religious events, love and sex.

The important point – worth repeating here – is that we all have the potential to have peak experiences, and it will be a personal matter as to which activities and situations might bring them to you.

As to how to find peak experiences, the advice on this is the same as that one might give to someone seeking happiness – don't seek it! Don't undertake activities simply because you feel they might bring you peak experiences, but just relax and do the things you enjoy that give you immersion, fulfilment and pleasure and if you get an occasional peak experience out of them, then great!

These experiences can be profoundly moving and mean a great deal to the people who have them. Overall they seem to give us an experience that is life-affirming – one in which we see what it is like to hit the heights of being alive.

Aside from the profound pleasure of the experience itself, peak experiences can bring a heightened sense of awareness, insight and understanding to people that might not otherwise have these things. This could be seen as a form of wisdom, and has the potential to bring us greater calm, and an outlook that has more perspective and is less self-centred.

ACTION

RECALL A PEAK EXPERIENCE – AND FIND MORE OF THEM

Try to recall an experience you've had that was special or where you were really concentrating on something and you felt great. Remember how you felt when you had the experience – did you feel immersed in it? What sensations and emotions did you feel? Did you have any thoughts at all? Then try to consider what it was about the experience that made it special - and how you might be able to find similar experiences again.

MINDFULNESS

Over the last 10 years or so, a mindfulness movement has emerged across the world that has made a lot of money out of people's desire for more reflective, peaceful lives in a busy and challenging world. You can get help with mindfulness from small local groups through to large global app and podcast providers.

But what is mindfulness and why does it matter? To quote the Life Squared publication 'The Inner Life', mindfulness is "the skill of paying attention, in particular to how our own inner life is operating, what habits are at work and how they are affecting what we think and feel. With this ability, we can begin to observe what stands in the way of inner peace and thus what stops us from being happy."[38]

It enables us to stand back from our thoughts and see ourselves as separate from them and able to control whether we engage with them or not. This is in contrast to feeling (as we often do) that we are controlled by our thoughts and that we must pay attention to, and be affected by, everything that comes into our heads. It helps us to realise that 'we are not our thoughts'.

Mindfulness helps us understand our relationship with our thoughts and control it better. It helps us identify any unhelpful habits we are engaging in. For example, it enables us to observe how anger arises in us, why we crave to eat or drink too much, what the patterns of thought are that deflate our confidence. Mindfulness is greater awareness of our own inner lives. It enables us to start shaping our inner habits into those that give us greater inner peace.

To quote Life Squared again: "since mindfulness consists of paying close attention to what is happening in the inner life it is best practiced by reminding yourself to observe and only observe. There are many ways of doing this. The best known practices are forms of meditation, for example those which try to focus attention on the breath." [39]

38   Wilkinson, Tony - The Inner Life, Life Squared, Lewes 2009
39   Wilkinson, Tony - The Inner Life, Life Squared, Lewes 2009

You don't need to be sitting still to practice mindfulness - you could do it by undertaking immersive physical activities such as running, yoga and martial arts and ensuring you give them your full, focussed attention without letting your mind wander. If your mind starts becoming distracted with other thoughts and feelings (which it often can), don't worry - just observe these and let them pass by, whilst returning your focus to the activity you're doing.

ACTION

TRY A MINDFULNESS PRACTICE

Find a quiet space and give yourself 20 minutes to try a simple meditation or mindfulness practice, such as focussing on your breathing going in and out. We will not set out detailed instructions here, but if you can, try out a real life class with a qualified instructor. If not, there are many free online courses, videos and apps for mindfulness and meditation - some provided by mental health charities. Remember it takes time and practice, so don't get frustrated or give up after your first attempt if you're finding it hard to quieten your mind during these initial sessions!

EXPLORING YOUR THOUGHTS

In the previous section, we considered how to develop a better relationship with your thoughts. Sometimes though, it's just nice to get immersed in them and float away with them, through daydreaming, imagination and reflecting on our memories.

In our hyper-busy society where economic productivity is king, it can be seen as lazy or inefficient to sit with our thoughts, but doing so can give us a great deal of pleasure and fulfilment, as well as being an essential tool for creativity.

Immersing ourselves within our thoughts should of course be an informed choice - a decision to dip in and dip out - as part of a better relationship with them and realising that we are not our thoughts, as discussed earlier. We can use it as a source of pleasure or creativity that we access when we want to, rather than something that distracts us or is unhelpful to us because we can't control our relationship with it.

You can do this 'mental grazing' anywhere at any time, and can be much more rewarding (and cheaper) than staring at a screen instead! You can pick at different thoughts as they float by, or make a conscious choice to access certain thoughts, such as memories, or build ideas in your imagination. We should recognise that neither memories nor the imagination may be an accurate reflection of the real world or the lives we've really lived, but they can give us comfort, pleasure and inspiration.

CONCLUSIONS – HOW TO EXPLORE YOUR INNER LIFE

For many people, exploration of their 'inner lives' (including reflective, experiential and spiritual matters) is one of the most profound and fulfilling aspects of life.

Many of us will not have given much thought to what 'life' actually is, or whether we are living with a particular interpretation of it. But most of us do seem to go through life with a subconscious view on it or interpretation of it, which can influence how we see and live our lives - so it's well worth checking whether our view of life is conducive to living well.

We can also gain a lot from taking some time to reflect on what it feels like to be alive. Thinking about all these things can add a real richness to our lives, as well as give us greater perspective and self awareness about our situation as living creatures.

To finish this chapter, listed below are a number of ways you can start to explore your inner life. They are simply practices, activities and habits that will enable you to put yourself into a good position to explore some of the areas discussed above. You'll no doubt be able to develop your own ideas and habits too - so have a think about those that put you into a relaxed state to reflect on these things.

1. **Have some daily reflection time** - give yourself at least ten minutes each day to sit quietly without disturbance, close your eyes, relax and clear your mind of thoughts. Feel what it is like to just exist. Activities such as meditation, yoga or walking in the countryside can help this process, but choose the way that suits you best.

2. **Savour your experiences** – whatever you are doing, savour the taste, touch, smell, sight and sound of your experiences, as well as the ongoing stream of consciousness and thought that enables you to think about all of this. Remember what it is like to be an 'experiencing' creature and remembering what it feels like to 'experience' anything. Keeping this in mind can give us a sense of wonder and appreciation in our lives that can really inspire us and improve our well-being.

3. **Be thankful** – regularly remind yourself about the remarkable fact that you exist, and are able to reflect on your experience of life. This doesn't have to be thanking anyone (like a god) in particular – it is just the process of acknowledging your luck in existing. This is an easy way to connect yourself with your inner world and feel more positive about daily life.

4. **Think about the big questions** - find some quiet time to think about issues such as the meaning of life, how the universe began and how you fit into the great scheme of things. The perspective you gain from this may well make you feel calmer in everyday life. Talk to your friends about these questions and see if you gain some new perspectives from each other.

5. **Learn** – read some books on philosophy, the history of thought and religion. Learn how to think in a clear way about philosophical matters. Learn about some of the issues that thinkers have grappled with over the centuries, think about them for yourself and come to your own conclusions.

6. **Explore other people's experiences** – discuss your ideas and experiences of your inner world with other people. Don't feel awkward about introducing these topics – most people enjoy talking about these issues when they get the chance. Doing this could help you develop your own ideas and bring you closer to the other people, by opening up a new side of yourselves to each other.

7. **Put your life into context** – look beyond the rush of daily life and start to see your life in a broader context - as part of a world population, a species, a natural world, a planet and a universe – and see if this changes the way you see your life.

8. **Look beyond daily life** - even when you are immersed within the complexity and grind of daily life, try to keep a slight sense of distance from it - a part of you that is standing back from it and reflecting on it, almost hovering above it, able to see at all times that you are just part of a story being acted out.

CHAPTER 6

HOW CAN I FIND MEANING IN MY LIFE?

*What are we seeking? — Thinking about meaning
— Obstacles to finding meaning — How to find
meaning — What gives us meaning?*

What is the meaning of life?

This is a question most of us have wrestled with at some point or another, and is perhaps the one that people have struggled with the most throughout the ages. A range of answers have been suggested – including 'Sex and drugs and rock and roll' and '42' (the latter courtesy of the great Douglas Adams) - but you may feel that neither of these provide a satisfactory answer for you.

In this chapter we will explore this question, and show how we can each find meaning in our lives. We will also briefly explore some of the common things that give people meaning.

WHAT ARE WE SEEKING?

Before we start, it will help if we can be clearer about what we are seeking when we ask ourselves what the meaning of life is. Is it really an answer to a simple question? What is 'meaning' anyway?

What we really seem to be asking when we pose questions such as 'what's the meaning of life' or 'what's the point of life?' is whether there is any particular purpose for which we are each alive.

And this is a massively important question for nearly all of us, even though we may choose to articulate it in different ways. To see how important it is, we only have to consider what it feels like (or would feel like) to be without a sense of purpose in life.

Many people can roll along through life just enjoying the experience of being alive, and as we will see, this is an important attitude to cultivate. But, at the same time, many of us also need to feel a sense of purpose to our lives - a reason for existing.

At its most extreme and tragic level, some people who feel a massive hole in their lives without a reason for existing decide they have no reason to continue living.

For some people, a lack of reason for existing can cause a sense of emptiness, a gaping hole in their lives that brings a sense of yearning to fill it. With an increasing sense of desperation to fill this void but no idea of how to do so, they may take a random, scattergun approach and try to fill it with anything they can, or find ways of trying to avoid thinking about it. Many of these options may not be what they really need and some - such as alcohol and drugs - may actually exacerbate their misery and sense of worthlessness.

So, finding meaning matters to us. We need a reason to get up every day rather than pull the covers over our head and stay in bed. We need to feel fulfilled and valued. We want a sense of identity and pride in who we are. We don't of course need a clear sense of purpose in our lives to feel a sense of value and pride in ourselves, but for many of us it certainly helps to make us feel like worthwhile human beings.

In some ways, it would be much easier if there was a clear answer to the question of why we exist. Especially if everyone's life had a very clear aim, which could be measured and it could be easily worked out if you'd achieved this aim or not.

Over the years, many people have sought to find clear answers to this question - and we can find ourselves living within cultures, nations, religions and political systems that contain quite specific views on what should give our lives meaning. As a result, we absorb these ideas and carry them with us as individuals, even though we may not realise it.

For example, political movements (from communism to liberalism) have sought to gain people's loyalty to a particular view of how the world should be, and each brings with it a view of what role each of us should play within this system - and hence, what gives meaning to our lives. This doesn't just apply to the more authoritarian political movements like communism. Even the market-driven liberal system we live under at the moment has a sense of what matters in life - namely, individual freedom, achieved through continuous economic growth and minimally regulated financial markets. This overarching priority 'trickles down' into our culture's dominant view of what's important in our individual lives, such as material success and career achievement.

Religions also carry assumptions about the meaning of life. At the most basic level, some monotheistic religions argue that the meaning of life is to live in a way that is pleasing to their god. Some religions promise a reward in the afterlife for doing this (see chapter 4 for more discussion on this). But even beyond this rather reductive level, religions have had an influence on what we each view to be meaningful, worthwhile lives. For example, influencing our ideas on how we should behave with regard to sexuality, work, ethics and many other areas.

All of these ideas and approaches have tried to argue that there is some objective reason or purpose for existence, and that following their ideas will enable you to find meaning. The problem is, there is no objective reason or purpose for existence.

And the 'meaning' that each of these ideologies offers - however convincing it may be - is ultimately just made up.

Any movement or ideology - whether political, religious or other - that claims to have found an objective reason is deluded. And, what's worse, it's making this claim of 'truth' at the expense of the infinite other ways of finding meaning or reason in life. It therefore cuts its followers or citizens off from these other ideas, or draws an arbitrary line in the sand that will inevitably cause conflict with other ideologies whose views differ from this. Any movement or ideology that claims to have knowledge of an objective truth in matters that are actually arbitrary opinion is a catalyst for conflict, persecution and human misery.

So, in one way it could be argued that many of these attempts to find clear answers to the question of meaning in life have been very successful, insofar as they have influenced billions of people to adopt their views of what matters in life. They may have been a great deal less successful for many of the people living within them however, as they have caused them immense anxiety and pain when trying to live in line with them - with ideas of meaning that aren't really their own, and being pressurised to follow particular views of life, without being given a chance to really think about what gives them meaning personally. The time has come for people to be able to think clearly about what really matters to them - without their views being completely moulded by the influence of others. The aim of this chapter is to help you do this by first challenging some of the assumptions overarching you about meaning in life.

It would be even more gratifying if one could identify a clear and specific objective aim that you - and only you - had in life. At its most extreme level, we can see how this sort of attitude could lead to an extreme level of self delusion or a messiah complex - the idea that you are the 'chosen one' to achieve a particular goal or aim. And that, as you have this clear sense of direction and others don't, you and your mission are therefore more important than other people. Individuals who have harboured delusions like this (and their followers) have been responsible for some of the great mistakes and horrors of human history.

THINKING ABOUT MEANING

So what is a more realistic way to think about meaning?

Let us begin with the brutal fact - as far as we know, life has no specific meaning. We are a group of life forms made of the same stuff as all the inanimate, lifeless objects in the universe. Life on Earth emerged by chance and a fortunate set of conditions, and we have evolved over billions of years to the creatures we are today. There is no great purpose to why we are here, despite what believers in the supernatural would have you believe.

Given this reality, the meaning of life is subjective - it is the meaning each of us attributes to our own life. So, we create the meaning in our own lives.

And although there is no objective, external meaning to our lives, there is plenty of meaning to be found within them, as conscious creatures with particular senses, instincts, needs and ideas. Later we will explore some of the things that might give us most meaning - as well as some of the things that don't seem to.

OBSTACLES TO FINDING MEANING

Many of the things that give us meaning are actually quite simple and sitting right in front of our eyes - for example, human relationships. We often find ourselves unable to see these things though, and can find ourselves wandering through life without a sense of meaning or struggling to find it whilst desperately seeking it. Our inability to find meaning in life could be for a number of reasons.

To start with, we may be searching for the wrong thing. Our search for meaning in life can be elusive if we become fixated on the idea of finding 'meaning' itself, as this doesn't exist as a specific thing - it is simply a made-up human concept. It will therefore slip through our fingers if we try to grab it. To find meaning, we have to focus on the things that give us meaning - not on the idea of meaning itself.

Another important reason why people might struggle to find meaning in their lives is that they are confused about what might give them meaning. This can be a particular challenge in the modern world, as there are many strong social, cultural and commercial influences encouraging us to seek meaning in certain things that don't actually bring much meaning for most people, such as wealth or material consumption, for reasons we discussed earlier in this chapter.

Take wealth, for example. Many people believe that having greater wealth brings greater happiness and fulfilment. So they sacrifice their lives striving for it. Yet, the evidence from comparing income and happiness levels of different countries shows that beyond a certain level of average wealth - around $20,000, according to Professor Richard Layard - "higher average income is no guarantee of greater happiness."[40] So, we're unlikely to find meaning simply in the pursuit of material wealth.

Yet the influences (such as advertising) that pedal these spurious ideas of meaning are extremely powerful, as they surround us in our daily lives, and represent 'reality' for many people. They can act as a fog that makes it harder for us to see what really gives us meaning, and can distract us with sparkly things that may give us short-term pleasure but fail to satisfy us or ultimately give us real meaning.

We can also end up constantly comparing our own lives with those of other people. This is not only unrealistic but can also be harmful to us as it can cause us stress and unhappiness when we fail to achieve these impossible goals. It is an ultimately unfulfilling approach anyway, as it is about what others have, not what we really want ourselves.

In the end, we should seek to make our own meaning in life - without being influenced by external forces.

The thinking tools we discuss in chapter 7 can play an important role in helping us to recognise the external influences on us and think clearly about what really matters to us.

40 Layard, Richard - Happiness - lessons from a new science, Penguin, London 2006, p.34

So, when you do the exercise at the end of this chapter to help you reflect on what gives you meaning, you need to be really honest with yourself about what matters to you and what gives you pleasure. Try to ignore the influence of wider society or what other people think - or indeed your own judgements of whether the priorities you come up with are 'worthwhile' or not - and just lay them out honestly. These will be your real priorities. Live in line with these and you won't go too far wrong, as you'll be living on your own terms.

HOW TO FIND MEANING

The solution is therefore for each of us to stand back from the influences and distraction around us, and be honest with ourselves about what really does give us meaning.

It's important to note that you don't have to be a philosopher in order to find meaning in life. You don't need to overthink this. You just need to be able to be honest with yourself about what gives you a sense of purpose, fulfilment and enjoyment in life. You don't have to emerge with any great, profound and snappy soundbite to describe it either - you can keep it in your head as a fluid, rough idea of what matters to you. And remember - you are answerable to no-one else for what gives you meaning in life, so don't try to judge your ideas against those of other people.

To help you identify what really matters to you, try this quick thought experiment. Imagine yourself in many years' time, lying on your deathbed. When you look back over your life what will be the things that gave you most meaning? Things you wished you'd given more time to?

Once you've gained a sense of what gives you meaning in life, you can then choose to live in a way that embraces it and is consistent with it. It's about living in line with your priorities - so that you can look back on a life well lived. This doesn't mean striving or setting yourself goals to live in line with what gives you meaning - it doesn't need to be a chore. It could simply be about choosing to do more of the things that give you meaning and fewer of the things that don't.

For example, if you spend most of your time at work but place a higher value on family life, try to redress the balance. There may be a number of ways you can do this, including changing your working hours, working from home more often or imposing a rule on yourself to not work at weekends or evenings.

WHAT GIVES US MEANING?

You will of course need to answer this question for yourself, but in this section we can summarise some areas that seem to provide meaning in many people's lives - no matter what their culture or background.

You'll notice in this section that we've not noted specific life goals (such as 'win the Nobel peace prize' or 'have three children'), even though they may be meaningful to some people. This is because setting goals for your life can be counterproductive, as you may not be in control of whether you achieve them or not (this applies to both examples above), and they leave you with potential to brand your entire life as meaningless or a failure if you've been unable to meet them. It can be fulfilling to continually challenge ourselves but basing our entire lives around goal fulfilment is likely to lead to disappointment and regret.

As discussed already, our lives are packed with potential sources of meaning as conscious, social creatures with particular senses, instincts, needs and ideas. With this in mind, some of the things that might give our lives meaning are:

- **Human relationships** - many people class their friendships, family and personal relationships as among the most important things in their lives. Yet it's amazing how much we can neglect or overlook them in favour of other things that give us less meaning.

- **Making a contribution** - doing things to help other people, participating in our communities or trying to make the world around us better provides many people with a great deal of fulfilment. It also enables them to feel they have left some sort of legacy once they have passed away.

- **Savouring the experience of life** - people use many terms to describe their particular ways of savouring the experience of life - including mindfulness, reflection and contemplation. But it ultimately boils down to some common ideas, such as the practice of contemplating our existence and acknowledging our sense of awe and wonder about it. We will explore these in more detail in chapter 9.

- **Pleasure** - it might seem frivolous to suggest this following such a reflective point, but experiences of pleasure can lend a great deal of meaning to our lives. From sensory pleasure - such as enjoying food or living in a warm climate - through to intellectual pleasures such as reading good books.

- **Creativity** - both the process of creativity and the completion of a creative project can be highly fulfilling. There is an almost boundless range of ways we can be creative, including cooking, writing, music, gardening and imagining.

- **Learning** - we are lucky enough to exist for 80 years or so, therefore one aspect of what it might mean to live a good life is to try to better understand the world around us and the life we are living. This could give us a greater sense of perspective, is using the intellectual faculties we have and could bring a richer existence to us during the time we are alive.

- **Applying ourselves** - applying ourselves, our concentration and our efforts to tasks and projects can give us a great sense of meaning and fulfilment - not just in the achievement or completion of the tasks themselves, but in the process of undertaking them in the first place. This could include learning a skill such as a language or musical instrument, or simply undertaking an intellectual task such as a crossword or reading a book.

- **Enjoying nature** - many people find that having a regular connection with nature is essential to the sense of fulfilment they get from life. This may be through walking in the countryside, stopping to appreciate a beautiful view or having a pet. It is another component of 'savouring the experience of life'.

- **Exercise** - there is great meaning to be gained from exercise of any sort. It can provide us with a chance to apply ourselves, experience nature, socialise and savour the experience of being alive - but above all can simply make us feel good - both physically and mentally, as well as improving our health in both the short and long-term.

As you can see from some of the ideas above, we don't need to don't need become philosophers and spend years wrestling with the abstract idea of the 'meaning of life' before we can actually get meaning from it. At the most basic level, if you simply enjoy your experience of life, you will have got meaning from it!

But if you want to think about it a bit further, take some quiet time to reflect on what gives your life meaning - and then build more of these things into your life, and try to worry less about the things that aren't on this list that you may have previously spent too much emotional energy on - for example, worrying about what you have achieved in relation to other people.

REFLECT ON WHAT GIVES YOU MEANING IN LIFE

Take yourself somewhere peaceful and quiet, perhaps in nature, away from the influence of other people. Have a think about what matters to you in life and what gives you pleasure. Try to consider this honestly, without judging yourself or wondering what other people might think about your choices. If you want to, write a short list (up to around 5) of these things. If you have time, perhaps also consider things that you've considered as priorities up to now that, upon reflection, have less meaning for you. Then consider how to build the real priorities into your life more - and release time on the old priorities to make more time for them.

CONCLUSIONS

Finding meaning is an important part of our individual lives. There is no objective 'meaning of life' - we need to find this for ourselves.

To help each of us identify what really gives us meaning in life, we need to challenge the assumptions about this issue that we have (often unwittingly and automatically) inherited from various ideologies, institutions and people around us over our lives. When we do this, and think for ourselves about what really matters to us, without judging these choices, we can live a life of greater meaning.

And this does not have to be a process of intellectual and personal struggle over a lifetime - we just need to reflect honestly about what matters to us in life, and then live in a way that prioritises these things.

CHAPTER 7

HOW CAN I THINK WELL?

Why does thinking matter? — 7 ways to think well

We all have brains. They're the most complex structures that we know of in the universe. And they don't just dominate our lives - they are our lives. Everything you see, think and experience is down to your brain.

But brains don't come with a user manual, and some people are more effective than others at using their brain to create a better life, and experience of life, for themselves. This chapter explores some of the key ways in which we can all do this - and think well.

As we'll see, the ability to see the world clearly and think well is one of the most important foundations for a wise and meaningful life. It can help us make better decisions and have a more fulfilling experience of life.

But what do we mean by 'thinking well'? It is a collection of skills, such as critical thinking, and attitudes, such as seeing the world with a sense of wonder and curiosity, that enable us to live our lives in a reflective and well-informed way, and to see the world with a reasonable level of perspective and clarity.

It's not just about thinking though - it's about managing our relationship with our thoughts. This includes understanding our tendencies to think in particular ways, and trying to adopt the ways of thinking that are most helpful to our well-being.

Before we start, here are a couple of arguments we are not trying to make in this chapter:

- We are not suggesting that human beings are simply 'thinking machines' that can or should use rational thought to optimize every aspect of their lives. The latest psychological research[41] shows that we are far less 'rational' than we might think, and that instinct often rules our behaviour and decision making. The fact remains however that we have the ability to refine or adapt our behaviour through the use of rational thought. So, it makes sense to use it in our lives when we can do so to our advantage.
- We're also not suggesting that we need to be spending our lives over-thinking or sitting in a state of reflection rather than actually taking action and getting on with our lives. Sometimes 'thinking well' may involve thinking more (for example, considering an important issue carefully) and other times it may mean thinking less (such as ignoring thoughts that are harming us or just leading us to procrastinate).

In this chapter we'll present some examples of what we mean by thinking well, and why these matter. It's not an exhaustive list, but a broad overview which should provide a useful set of initial ideas you can put into action. In chapter 9 'How to get the most out of life' we will set out some further ideas on how you can manage your mental health and improve your experience of life.

41 For example, 'Thinking, Fast and Slow', Daniel Kahneman, Penguin London, 2011

WHY DOES THINKING MATTER?

Before we ask how we can think well, we should ask why we need to think well - why this matters in the first place.

IT IS GOOD TO LIVE A CONSIDERED LIFE

We suggest that a considered life is better than an unconsidered one. Below is a quote from John Stuart Mill, father of the philosophical idea of Utilitarianism, that famously sums up this point:

> *"It is better to be a human being dissatisfied than a pig satisfied; better to be Socrates dissatisfied than a fool satisfied. And if the fool, or the pig, are a different opinion, it is because they only know their own side of the question."*[42]

The argument runs like this. It's quite possible to be perfectly happy with an unconsidered life in which you don't think deeply about anything and never challenge yourself. But a more considered life could be better, because:

- An unconsidered life is a restricted and limited one. The pleasures and fulfilment you gain from the more considered life could be more profound than those from the unconsidered life.
- Even a considered life that contains pain and difficulty could be ultimately more fulfilling than one that's unconsidered.
- In an unconsidered life, you simply don't know what you're missing out on. Even if you don't know or care about what you're missing, there's a significant cost to your life in terms of 'opportunity missed'.
- A considered life enables you to use more of your potential as a human being. We have the ability to live a considered life, so let's use it.

42 Mill, John Stuart - Utilitarianism, 1863

Notice that we don't say 'a considered life is more valuable than an unconsidered one'. This is not for us - or anyone - to say. Both lives are equally valuable, as all human lives are of equal value.

IT IS GOOD TO LIVE A WELL-INFORMED LIFE

We also suggest that a well-informed life is better than an ill-informed one. There are a number of reasons for this.

Perhaps the most obvious one is that being well-informed helps you to make better decisions. As we argued at the start of this book, by learning, and passing this learning on to each other, human beings have been able to not only increase our life expectancy but also build our knowledge and develop our society to where it is today. By relying on solid, reliable information rather than luck we increase our chances of success in most endeavours - not just life or death situations. For example, imagine you're about to buy a seond-hand car. Out of two seemingly identical looking cars, one could turn out to be a bargain and the other a banger. You can give yourself the best chance of making a good decision (and not wasting money, your life and those of other people) if you get informed about each car's history and what's under their bonnet.

Following on from one of the arguments for a considered life, a well-informed life could open up more possibilities and greater fulfilment for you. For example, by learning that the country of Papua New Guinea exists and about the landscape and species that live there, you are presented with somewhere new you may wish to visit, which could add something to your life.

Gaining new knowledge and discovering new things is rewarding in itself.

When human beings live well-informed lives it can also improve wider society. This is an important point. For example, if more people learn about the danger of climate change and how they can take action to reduce their impact, we stand a better chance of addressing the issue globally. Or, at a time of a virus pandemic, if more people know how to prevent spreading the virus (and take action to do it), this will help to reduce the spread.

IT HELPS US TO BE FREE AND LIVE OUR OWN LIVES (AS MUCH AS IT'S POSSIBLE TO)

We all like to believe that we are in control of our own actions and thoughts. As we have seen from earlier chapters though, in reality this is far from the case.

We are much more vulnerable to manipulation than we think, especially when we live in a complex world where we are surrounded by a vast array of influences on our thinking and behaviour, including advertising, peer group pressure and many other things.

If we don't learn to think for ourselves (as much as our natural makeup will allow us to), we can risk living lives where we are just thinking the thoughts and following the behaviours that other people have instilled in us. And if you look around in the modern world, you can see this happening everywhere. Just as one example, think of the vast amounts of time, effort and money people spend to keep up and fit in with their peers in how they look and what they own.

If we live our lives just carried along by other people's ideas and values, without questioning them, this is not freedom - it's a form of mental slavery. So, thinking for ourselves matters if we are to carve out our own lives for ourselves.

THINKING IS ENJOYABLE

Aside from these more abstract arguments, there's the simple point that thinking is enjoyable. This doesn't necessarily have to be the high-level, complex thinking required by philosophy (although this is certainly very enjoyable for many of us!) but could simply be the day to day process of reflecting on life and the things that come up in it.

We tend to denigrate the idea of reflection, using the pejorative term 'daydreaming' to describe some types of abstract and creative thought, but this is only because we live in a society obsessed with money, productivity and time, and anything that doesn't immediately seem productive is slammed. But broad reflecting activities like this can be both enjoyable and incredibly rewarding, resulting in new ideas, creativity and insights that we might not have otherwise had. Perhaps if the world had more daydreamers we'd have better lives - and a better world.

CONCLUSIONS – WHY THINKING MATTERS

There are some powerful reasons why a reflective, informed approach to life is important. This does of course need to be balanced with a desire to take action and get on with living, as it is good to take action and not just reflect.

But we live in a speed-driven, turbo-capitalist world where action dominates and instant gratification is king - leading to short term thinking, harmful actions being taken without enough thought, and opinions offered without any real consideration. In this atmosphere, reflection and consideration can be dismissed as navel gazing, as laziness. But we would argue that reflection and consideration can be dynamic activities and should be seen as a key part of taking action, and of living well. Ultimately we could use a lot more reflection in the modern world.

7 WAYS TO THINK WELL

In the section below we have set out seven ways you can think well. These are primarily based on building your thinking skills, but also include a final point on how to manage the thoughts that run through your brain.

1. GAIN PERSPECTIVE ON YOUR LIFE

Within the rush of everyday life, it can be easy to lose sight of the big picture surrounding your own existence – including the fact that you are materially better off than the vast majority of other people, living or dead, you are simply another member of the animal kingdom and you are just one of 7.7 billion human beings living on a tiny planet in a vast universe.

It is useful to be able to see the big picture on a wide range of topics, a few of which we will outline below. Understanding issues such as how we got to this point in history, how people work and how our ideas work can all help us to adopt a broader, wiser, more considered approach to life.

So, take some time to stand back from your life and take yourself on a learning journey to explore the big picture, including:

The universe – understanding the sheer scale of the universe, from the massive to the minute, can provide us with a sense of awe, put a more realistic spin on our problems and worries, make us feel part of a bigger picture (whether it is human beings, the natural world or the universe generally) and give us a more modest sense of our own self-importance.

Our planet – building an overview of the rich diversity of the planet's terrain, animals, plant life and makeup can help us appreciate the wonder of life on Earth, and give us greater motivation to protect it.

Human life – gaining a picture of your place in relation to the other people on the planet will help you to appreciate the massive differences in wealth, lifestyles, education and life opportunities across this population, and how lucky you are in relation to the vast majority of them. It could also lead to a better understanding of the varied cultures and beliefs around the world, and could therefore promote greater empathy.

Philosophy, history and politics – gaining an insight into philosophy, history and politics could give you perspective on the history of ideas, not only understanding those that have defined people's lives and societies throughout history (in areas from religion to politics), but also how they have evolved and fallen in and out of favour. It will also help you question some of the ideas and institutions overarching our lives today - from neoliberal economics to the idea of moral progress - and give you a better appreciation of the alternatives.

These are just a few of the most important areas you could choose to explore, and this book hopefully makes a contribution to building this perspective. Ultimately, embarking on a learning journey and developing a sense of broad perspective like this could be one of the most personally rewarding things you will ever do.

2. BASE YOUR DECISIONS AND VIEWS ON EVIDENCE

We have already explored some reasons why it pays to live a well-informed life, and there are similar reasons why you should base your decisions and views on evidence.

Quite simply, using evidence means we are striving to recognise reality as accurately as possible when we live our lives, which in turn gives us the firmest foundations to base our lives on.

So, how can we use evidence more to inform our lives? Here are a few ideas:

Keep learning - it sounds like a simple point, but by maintaining a sense of curiosity about the world and continuing to read and learn about it, you will be accumulating more evidence to help you base your ideas and decisions on.

Get into the habit of seeking evidence - not just before you act, but before you decide to absorb or accept any piece of information you encounter. This is simply part of thinking critically and adopting an attitude of 'curious scepticism' towards the world. For example, if you read a newspaper article claiming that watching television causes cancer, before you decide to absorb this and place it on the shelf in your head labelled 'facts', ask what the evidence is for this claim, see if you can find it and ask yourself whether it stacks up. Or is there more reliable evidence pointing to a different conclusion?

Remember, a newspaper article is often not itself a source of evidence - it is a carrier and interpreter of information - some of it reliable, some not. The same applies to other media channels. You need to identify the source of their claim - the piece of academic research, a piece of investigative journalism, the survey by a PR company etc. Finding the most robust sources of evidence will help you work out whether a piece of information is reliable or not.

Learn how to identify reliable sources of evidence - our sources of evidence matter. So far, we have been talking about the need to seek evidence, but perhaps we need to be more specific - we need to seek reliable evidence.

In a world where we can find anything at the touch of an internet search button it might seem very easy to seek evidence. But, as we will see in the later point of 'information literacy', not all sources of evidence are equal. We have to find the right, robust evidence – not the stuff that's easiest to find or the echo chambers that back up our own views – such as Donald Trump's reliance on the biased right-wing broadcasting of Fox News as his main news source.

Some sources (like Fox News) purport to provide evidence but actually just offer opinion or a biased interpretation of the evidence, so we need to find some trusted sources of information for whatever evidence we are seeking.

Finding reliable sources of evidence involves a bit more work than just accepting the first thing you read, but it doesn't have to be an onerous process, as you can quickly develop an understanding of the sort of sources that will be reliable and those that won't.

There are a range of factors that can help you judge whether a piece of evidence is robust or not - for example, whether it was from a respected source such as a known university, whether the body publishing the evidence has a political bias (like a think tank), whether a survey was sponsored by a company in order to sell a product. It will also help if you question why a particular information source (such as a particular newspaper) might choose to adopt a particular position on this issue - for example, if it's known to have a political bias, if an article has been placed by a PR agent, or some other reason. See the later section on 'critical thinking' for more guidance on this.

Don't spread misinformation - human beings love communicating. But we can all play a part in making a better world by keeping quiet sometimes and refraining from communication. We live in the days of social media where information can travel among millions of people almost instantly. This has some great advantages for human flourishing but also creates some challenges - one of which is that some pieces of information can spread quickly and stimulate emotions and behaviour in people like a virus - whether it is accurate or not. A negative or inaccurate piece of information can spread just as quickly as a positive or accurate one. We therefore each need to take personal responsibility for the information we are spreading - as each of us is a hub that influences other people, and by not communicating inaccurate information, we are stemming its spread to others.

During the coronavirus crisis, we saw many examples of why it's important to refrain from spreading misinformation, as worried people spread rumours and misinformation about all sorts of things, from the origins of the virus to shortages of certain products. At the simplest and perhaps least important level, this led to the stockpiling of completely random items such as toilet rolls - a change in behaviour across millions of people, motivated by an emotion (fear), triggered simply by the spread of information - and information based on no, or very poor, evidence. And there are many more serious examples of the effects of spreading misinformation happening every day.

So, play your part in stopping misinformation from spreading - and the anxiety, fear and other consequences that can come from it - by thinking about what you say, and sometimes just saying nothing. This doesn't just apply to your behaviour on social media but in every area of daily life, from social situations to the workplace. We are often tempted to communicate in order to fit in, show our status or demonstrate we are contributing to a discussion - but resist this temptation if it means contributing to the spread of misinformation.

Challenge misinformation - following from the previous point, we should be willing to challenge misinformation when we see or hear it, if we think it could be useful to do so. But remember you are challenging the evidence that information or opinion is based on, so be sure to use evidence to counter the argument, otherwise your argument is no better than the one you're challenging. Also, you're not trying to win an argument or get 'one over' on another person, so don't just attempt to shout louder than the other person, try to humiliate them or resort to personal insults. People won't begin to consider alternative evidence if it feels like you are undermining them personally.

3. THINK FOR YOURSELF

Earlier in this chapter, we mentioned how our thoughts and actions are influenced by many external factors, including advertising, peer group pressure and many other things.

In an extraordinarily complex world in which we're surrounded by influences, complexity and distractions, we need to learn how we're influenced by the wider world, how to challenge the information we receive (whether this is broad ideas or individual messages), how to filter out the stuff that is biased and irrelevant to us and how to locate the golden nuggets of relevant, credible information that we actually need.

In other words, we need to learn how to think for ourselves. Unfortunately many of the skills we need to do this aren't taught to us in our early lives, so we end up living without these tools and become even more vulnerable to manipulation from, and confusion about, the outside world in our adult lives. Whilst we do of course need to start teaching these important skills more in our education system, we can also each do something to develop them in ourselves as adults.

Read my book 'The Life Trap' for the full picture on how we can think in a better informed, more independent way and why it matters so much, both to our ability to live good, fulfilled lives as individuals, and our ability to build a good, civilised society.[43]

Here are some of the key features of thinking for ourselves:

Understanding how our minds work - we should each try to gain some 'mental self awareness' by developing a basic picture of how human beings think and behave. We explored this briefly in chapter 3. As a species we are at an early stage of our understanding on this, and we should acknowledge this with humility, but understanding the basics of the latest neurological and psychological research can help us our tendencies for thinking and behaving in particular ways, and our vulnerabilities - for example, to manipulation by others. This in turn can help us live in a way that is aware of, and adapts to, these biases, and could help us both improve our lives and make society more compassionate and civilised.

Understanding how the world affects us - we should aim to develop an understanding of how our views and behaviour can be influenced and the common ways this can happen in our modern lives. This includes understanding the various ways in which we can be influenced, and the techniques that can be used - such as 'framing' - by others to influence us. Another part of this skill is being aware of the manifold channels through which these influences could reach us, from broader things such as social pressure and political language, through to individual messages such as advertisements. In the next sections of this chapter we'll look at these in more detail, including three ways we can address these challenges - through media literacy, political literacy and information literacy.

43   Docwra, Richard - The Life Trap, Lfe Squared, Lewes 2018

Critical thinking - this is the art of questioning the ideas and messages that we receive from any external source - whether it is friends, newspapers, television, the internet, or anything else. This isn't confined to specific messages such as advertisements or conversations but also broader cultural, political, or social orthodoxies such as the importance of striving for ever greater material wealth. We'll talk about this a bit more now.

Critical thinking is both a skill and an attitude towards the world. An attitude not of suspicion but of curiosity and scepticism - a desire to challenge whatever you are told until you can assure yourself that it is genuine. A commitment to not just accepting what you're told.

There are many things we can't control in the world around us. But by learning how to think critically, we start to impose some personal control where it really matters. It means we think for ourselves, rather than being carried along by the tide – whether this is of other people's opinions or the influence of those with wealth and power.

A central aspect of critical thinking is to challenge everything that we see or hear - whether it's the ideas and values our parents or religious teachers instilled in us, or the overarching priorities of the political and economic system that surround us. We should challenge it all. Sometimes you won't even realise you are surrounded by certain assumptions, as they are so 'baked into' our lives and mindsets. For example, the idea that achieving material wealth is the sign of a successful life, or that a working day should be 9-5.

Challenging these things requires some ongoing vigilance but it doesn't have to lead to exhausting paranoia! It's about cultivating an ongoing sense of 'curious scepticism' about the world around us. In other words, wanting to find out more about a particular message or idea, and being open to the possibility it could be useful and have been sent with positive intentions, rather than assuming every message has been sent to us with manipulative, negative intent. And, for messages that we do identify to be biased or unreliable in some way, having the humility to understand why they might have got this way and whether some positive or useful content can be found in them, rather than just dismissing all 'imperfect' messages as evil and biased.

For example, many non-religious people might view certain religious texts as factually and historically inaccurate, attempting to influence people not to think for themselves but instead to adopt a restricted, arbitrary view of the world and responsible for bringing about oppression and suffering. These criticisms are true to some extent, but dismissing religious texts entirely because of this may stop us understanding them better or seeing the value they can have. Perhaps we could make our view of them more nuanced by acknowledging their faults, but then recognising that they were written a long time ago when our knowledge of the world wasn't as advanced as it is now, and seeing them as attempts to make sense of the world, and how to live good lives within it. This doesn't mean we should believe or follow them, but we should be willing to show some understanding and humility to the ideas and messages we're choosing to reject, as well as towards the people who hold them.

We should extend this sense of 'curious scepticism' so that we habitually challenge everything we hear or see - no matter how powerful their source (appeals to authority - such as 'your parents are always right') or how long these ideas have been held (appeals to tradition - such as 'long-held religious or cultural ideas are right').

4. DEVELOP YOUR MEDIA LITERACY

In the modern world, we each have access to a wider range of ways of consuming information and communications than ever before, including books, televisions, mobile phones, computers and much more. We need to learn how to integrate these different areas into our lives in a way that enhances rather than threatens the fulfilment we get out of them.

Each of these channels fires a vast range of communications towards us. With such an overwhelming array of messages reaching us every day, it is particularly important that we each get into the habit of questioning any messages we receive, so that we can evaluate whether the sources are reliable, what the purpose of the message is, how we should interpret it, and whether it is something to be digested or ignored. For example, many of the messages we encounter in our lives have been produced to encourage us to buy particular products, yet this can be done in subtle ways and we need to develop an awareness of where messages have bias like this.

This act of questioning and evaluating these things could be described as 'media literacy'. Below are a few simple ways you can build yours:

Develop a balanced 'mind diet' - these days, we're not only eating things that are bad for our physical health, but we're also doing things that are making our minds flabby, rather than nurturing them. For example, the average person in the UK spends three and a half hours per day watching television! By feeding our mind like this, we can end up with a restricted view of the world. We can also lose sight of real life, feel bad about ourselves and forget to live our own lives. There are many things we could do to improve our mind diet, and make our lives more interesting, happy and wise in the process.

For example, many people spend a lot of time in front of screens - from mobile phones to TVs. Although there's nothing wrong with these things in moderation, it's easy to let them take over our lives and distract us from important things or make us feel less inclined to do them - including reading, seeing friends, exercising - the list goes on. This doesn't mean you have to stop watching TV or reading gossip magazines - as with food, what we're looking for is a good, balanced diet. Perhaps we should think of books as the 'fruit and vegetables' of our mind diet.

ACTION

THINK ABOUT YOUR 'MIND DIET'

For one week, keep a media diary to review how much time you spend using different media channels, including social media, TV, newspapers and books. Is it balanced - or are particular channels (such as social media and TV) stopping you from doing other things and living more fully? If so, set yourself a time limit to spend on these channels each week, and see how you get on by continuing your media diary for a few more weeks!

Think critically about the messages you receive - we need to take a different view of the media that surround us. Instead of trusting everything we read, watch or hear, we need to adopt a sceptical, critical attitude towards them.

This is because a significant proportion of the messages we receive will be biased in some way. For example, if you read a newspaper article telling you about the amazing properties of a new medical cure, this could have been placed by a PR company trying to promote that product. Or, a particular broadcaster's coverage of a news event may have a political bias to it that skews its interpretation of the facts. Even the messages we receive from our friends, schools and workplaces could have biases, perhaps stemming from beliefs or dogmas overarching our society (such as the the need for material and career success) or from particular aims that these contacts might want these messages to achieve with us (for example, workplaces trying to make us more productive).

These types of 'warped' messages are everywhere around us, but they don't have to be overwhelming for us - we can manage our relationship with them.

In our everyday consumption of media, we need to get into the habit of informing ourselves about the sources and biases of the media we consume and take this into account when we interpret and consume them.

When you receive any message, whether it is in a social conversation, at work, in a newspaper, or on television, think about whether you want to accept it or not. You may decide to ignore a particular message because you don't feel the topic is important or because you feel its view of a topic is too biased. Consider the source it came from and whether it might have a particular agenda.

If you feel a particular message or source is too biased, you may want to get a more balanced view of the topic by exploring messages from a few different sources with different perspectives (for example, looking at the same story in other newspapers) or by finding a source you can trust before you make a judgement.

ACTION

IDENTIFY THE INFLUENCES AROUND YOU

As you go about your day over the next few hours, try to evaluate each of the messages you see, hear or receive, from every source, including TV, internet, friends and your workplace. Go through the steps noted in the section above for each message to consider its purpose, source, bias and whether you want to accept it or ignore it. At the end of the day, reflect upon how many of the messages you've needed to challenge in some way, and how you can adjust your habits when interpreting messages from all sources from now on.

Live a good life online - the rise of digital technology, including mobile phones and digital media, has transformed our lives in the last couple of decades. This has brought many positive changes for us, but has also brought a range of challenges that many people are still trying to adjust to.

These include how to keep children safe online, maintaining the privacy and security of our data and navigating the complexity of the internet so that we can see what information is reliable and what isn't. This is a big, wide-ranging issue and there are too many points to discuss in detail here, although we will cover the issue of information literacy in a later section. Instead, we will set out some broad principles to help you think about the online world and how to navigate it:

See the online world as part of the real world - although we tend to separate them in our minds, it is helpful to see the digital world as very much part of the 'real' world. It is a place where people seek information (like a library), buy things (like a shop), have conversations (like a town square or park) or do many other things that they'd do in the 'real world'. And most importantly, at the heart of it all is still human beings interacting with each other. The online world is therefore simply a different place where these things happen.

Adopting this attitude helps us cut through the complexity of the online world and adopt similar attitudes and behaviours to those we'd apply to the real world. For example, the tone of communications on social media between people can be far more confrontational and aggressive than it would be in person. Although we may be inclined to behave differently in online conversations when we have a level of anonymity, we should treat other people in them with the same values and sense of respect that we would in the real world.

It can be hard to see the online world as part of the real world when so much of the online world is unseen by us and its workings take place behind the scenes. When we don't understand it, it is easy to see a threat in the online world - that it is dangerous and shadowy. And of course, in places it is - just like the 'real' world. But if we can become a bit more familiar with how it works, we can take more of the opportunities it offers, whilst being alert to the threats it poses.

Get better informed about the digital world - this point follows from the previous one. Taking the time to understand the digital world and how it affects our lives will help us to take control of our lives, security and data online. Doing this can increase our confidence in exploring the online world and encourage us to make more of its potential to enhance our lives.

We also need to become better informed about the online world in order to protect our data - a commodity that has become increasingly valuable to companies, governments and other parties. In the last couple of decades, the 'digital world' has moved far beyond our computer screens and into many other aspects of our lives - including mobile phones, watches, cars and home thermostats. Each of these items, and many more, is capable of extracting a rich range of data about our identity and behaviour, with much of it then being used as a valuable resource by these organisations, to be analysed and traded in order to target advertising at us.

Many people are not aware of information on us that technology firms are able to tap into from even seemingly simple apps, devices or searches. Nor do they know what this data is used for, or what they are actually signing away when they click 'accept' on the terms and conditions of an app without reading them - and many are effectively unreadable as they are so long and complex.

This is already an important global issue and is only going to get bigger. So, keeping better informed about the digital world is not just about being able to avoid online scams - it also helps us understand the 'new rules of engagement' that many companies and other bodies have developed without us noticing but with our unwitting consent. We need to take back control of the personal data that we generate, and the data trails we leave behind.

5. DEVELOP YOUR INFORMATION LITERACY

We live in a complex world where we are saturated with information.

First, there is a massive amount of information out there, and it's growing - fast. Most of the world's data has been created in the last few years, and the global market intelligence firm IDC predicts the world's data will grow to 175 zettabytes in 2025. A number of this scale might be meaningless on its own - but to put it in context:

- "If you were to store 175 zettabytes on DVDs, your stack of DVDs would be long enough to circle Earth 222 times.
- If you attempted to download 175 zettabytes at the average current internet connection speed, it would take you 1.8 billion years to download."[44]

There is an endless supply of information out there but we have limited time in our lives to consume it. Most of this information will be of little use to you personally, and one challenge we face is to not waste our time on all the irrelevant information that's out there. This is more difficult than you might think as the whole raison d'etre of much of the content on the internet is to grab our attention - otherwise no-one would view it. Companies and other information providers spend (and make) billions of dollars by finding ever more effective ways of grabbing our attention even when we weren't planning to give it.

We need to give ourselves the choice of how we want to prioritise the time in our lives, and what we want to give our attention to - rather than this choice being made for us.

We therefore need to find ways to take control of our relationship with the internet, our screens and the information on it. This includes developing a more balanced 'mind diet' as noted earlier, and also by becoming more aware of how our unconscious behaviour is being affected by our devices and the

44 www.bernardmarr.com/default.asp?contentID=1846

web. For example, perhaps you habitually turn to your mobile phone to check messages or browse the web the moment you run out of stimulation (e.g. when the friend you are meeting in the cafe goes to the toilet), or when you find yourself going down a tunnel of clicking links on the internet for an hour when you had only meant to quickly visit one site.

ACTION

MONITOR YOUR UNCONSCIOUS SCREEN HABITS

For the rest of the day, identify the moments when your attention wants to wander towards your screen or towards the internet. It might be when you're at work, waiting for someone, queuing for a bus - but just try to identify how often this occurs and how habitual this reaction is. Then, put in place some alternative habits to take back control - such as only checking your emails twice a day, turning off your wifi when working or giving people your full attention in conversations.

Another challenge is how to find the right information when we are actually looking for something. Even when we are seeking a particular piece of information, there is likely to be a wide range of sources purporting to show this information, but many could be biased, inaccurate or irrelevant.

So, a really important skill we need to develop when seeking information is to know how to 'find the needle in a haystack'. In other words, to know how to search not only for the most relevant information you need, but also the most reliable sources of this information within an almost endless mass of possible information. For example, you don't just want any old information about how to reduce your CO_2 emissions, but the most reliable and credible information on this.

Before the modern information age, libraries and books used to be the most obvious way of finding information. And they remain a useful source. In the modern world though, most people would turn to internet search engines to seek information. These can be incredibly useful, but, as we've seen, they are subject to their own algorithms and biases which can obscure the pieces of information we are really seeking. So, we need to know where to look and how to use information sources as effectively as possible.

This might sound like an onerous, time-consuming task, but once you get into some new habits and start building an understanding of what your trusted sources of information might look like, this process of being better-informed can become second nature to you.

Here are some initial ideas on how you can develop the process of finding good sources of information. Needless to say, these are just a broad, initial guide. Whatever source of information you encounter - even one that you trust - you should never stop looking at it with a critical, 'curiously sceptical' eye.

Use trusted international institutions - for example the World Health Organisation or United Nations. These can be reliable sources of facts about the world, as well as sources of credible research. National institutions (for example the NHS in the UK or the CIA World Factbook in the US) can also provide access to credible information, but greater caution should be exercised with these as their tone and messaging can be influenced by the political and policy biases of the current government of that country.

Search scientific papers - these tend to use credible processes, from rigorous scientific method to peer review, to put their information together. We should get used to consulting these, as they aren't as scary and unapproachable as they seem, and can help us become better informed about topics. Google Scholar is a good way to search for these papers. Write 'review' in your search along with the topic you're looking for, as this will help you find articles that review a range of research and help you find the most reliable pieces.

Go to primary sources - for example, if a newspaper article is quoting a survey result that gives a particular piece of information, find that original survey. Then consider its reliability - for example - Was it developed by a reliable source? Did they use reliable methods such as sample sizes? Was it commissioned or sponsored by a company to sell something or promote a particular viewpoint?

Use fact checking sites - these can be useful to help you separate bias from facts (particularly in political matters), as they do some of the fact checking on your behalf. These include Factcheck and Snopes.

Seek reliable websites with less bias - as you'll be aware, websites vary in their reliability. Steer away from companies who are trying to sell you things as their information may be biased. Some educational, health and not-for-profit institutions may have a mission to provide credible information. Seek good journalism - it does still exist, and find the reports and stories that seek to uncover the facts, but take into account any biases they or their publishers might have. Exercise caution with individual bloggers and sites - but try to understand their background and credibility. Wikipedia can be useful - but exercise caution if there is a warning at the top of the page.

6. DEVELOP YOUR POLITICAL LITERACY

We encounter politics every day in our lives - including people's opinions, the newspapers we read and the feelings we have about how the world should be. Politics has a massive influence on whether our lives turn out to be flourishing or suffering - so it's another important area that we need to learn how to navigate and interpret the messages we receive.

There is a sense of cynicism about politics in the modern age, but many politicians, campaigners and people generally are still motivated by a genuine desire to make the world a better place. There however a couple of reasons why we have to be vigilant when interpreting messages from other people and sources about politics.

First, each person's (including each politician's) view of what could make the world a better place can vary a great deal - both in terms of the values they believe in (e.g. 'our country should offer a safe haven to refugees') and how they think these values can most effectively be put into action (e.g. 'we should let refugees stay in the UK for 5 years').

Our values can be hard to get a grip on sometimes, as morality doesn't consist of clear boundaries between 'right' and 'wrong'. In truth, it is a collection of grey areas and questions of degree - and no-one has the 'right' answer, because there rarely is one in the field of morality. See chapter 10 for more discussion of what values are.

Politicians, and anyone who talks about politics, therefore have a choice. They can either admit that values are grey areas on a spectrum, and engage in an honest conversation about these values with other people, in an attempt to find compromise and the best solution to an issue. Or they can simply attempt to convince people that their view is the 'right' one, through blocking attempts to discuss the issue properly and refusing to accept that values can have grey areas. The extent to which people do this varies in everyday life, but it will be clear to you which of these is the norm in modern politics!

Second, each politician, or individual or organisation involved in politics, needs and seeks to gain some form of influence and power (and then retain it) if they are going to be successful in their aims to make the world better - in whatever sense they see it. This is the case no matter what their political views are. And this can make them prone to putting a spin on facts to suit the messages they want to get across.

In summary, politics is an area in which the aim is to influence and convince - rather than necessarily to communicate information in a clear, understandable and unbiased way. This means that, when we are encountering any messages related to politics, we need to have our critical thinking faculties primed and ready, as they are likely to have work to do in order to get to the bottom of what's being said and why.

Listed below are some of the techniques that politicians (or anyone else discussing politics) might use to influence us, win an argument or convince us that their views are right. All of them involve trying to distract our attention from the core of their actual argument and the values at the heart of it - which is the valuable stuff you really want to get to, so you can understand and engage with them on it. It is also, however, the stuff that is harder to 'win' an argument with, as it is more about the longer process of discussion, understanding each other and reaching a common ground on grey areas than quickly 'winning' an argument based on black and white positions.

So, many people who are seeking a quick 'win' for their arguments - like some politicians - will aim to put a shell of certainty around their arguments to help win them. What you need to do is crack open this shell of certainty and expose the real assumptions and values at the centre of it. Understanding some of the techniques they use to build this shell will help us do this. These include:

Moral certainty - politicians are fond of moral certainty. You will often hear the phrase 'This is the right thing to do'. In a political world where we are being asked to follow orders from up high, it's easy to see why they use this language, as it gives voters a sense that the politician is in control, is powerful, is able to make clear decisions and take decisive action.

Unfortunately though, statements like this are also false, and can negatively affect us. As we've already seen, morality and values are a collection of grey areas and questions of degree - and no-one has the one 'right' answer, because there rarely is one in morality. But by claiming that their view is 'The right thing to do', a politician attempts to stop debate, close down any other moral possibilities than their own and make you accept their view. This is clearly either naive, or manipulative, misleading and dishonest. So always be distrustful of a politician who says 'this is the right thing to do' because it's never that simple.

Over-simplification - following on from the previous point, there can be a broader tendency in politicians when communicating with the public to over-simplify issues - not just moral choices - and reduce them to black or white debates. For example, the political campaigns that led up to the 2016 EU membership referendum in Britain failed to communicate the detail of an immensely complicated and important issue, and instead reduced the issue to vastly over-simplified, and often inaccurate, claims and accusations.

Politicians from all sides can get sucked into an over-simplistic blame game on issues such as this, instead of trying to openly address the complexities and issues it presents and trying to actually solve the problem. Some of the reasons for this type of stance could be a fear of publically 'losing face', a desire not to make issues complicated for the public and a desire to keep their 'political message' clear on each issue.

In reality though the world is a complex place, and it is important for us to understand this, so that we have realistic expectations of other people (including politicians) and our own aspirations for the society we want to see. Also, if we, as the public, were able to develop a better understanding of the complex issues that politicians must wrestle with, it could make us empathise more with them and feel more positively towards them.

Not answering questions - politicians are given media training to enable them to move any interviews or TV appearances to their own agenda as soon as possible. This can take a number of forms.

First, they might simply ignore the question they've been asked, and pivot to the issue they want to discuss e.g. 'What is the government going to do about the train drivers' strike?' could be answered with 'Well, I think the most critical issue today is the latest employment figures which show...'.

Another tactic is to fail to give a direct answer to the question. Next time you listen to a politician being interviewed, notice that they almost never reply 'yes' or 'no' to an answer. This enables a politician to switch the question to the point they want to make, and also means they avoid making commitments or statements that they might have to stick to at a later date.

This is most famously illustrated by Newsnight presenter Jeremy Paxman's infamous interview with the then home secretary Michael Howard, in May 1997. Paxman asks Howard the question "Did you threaten to overrule him?" - and Howard deliberately avoids answering the question. Frustrated at not getting a straight answer, Paxman asks the same question again, and is met with the same evasion. In the end, he asks the same question twelve times and fails to receive a direct answer.

These tactics from politicians are all incredibly frustrating for us as viewers and members of the electorate as they make us feel as if they aren't speaking to us honestly, are blocking communications and are deliberately trying to manipulate the truth. It turns political discourse into a stodgy, unedifying mess. No wonder many people have become cynical about politicians and politics.

Refusing to admit error - there is a well-known tendency among modern politicians to 'spin' their communications - to present information in a particular way that will suit their point of view. This can run from emphasising the positives in disappointing budget figures through to simply refusing to admit errors. This can lead to the public having a very unclear view of how their country or local council is being run, with facts being obscured from us.

This particular method of influencing seems to stem from a politician's desire to seem 'strong' to voters and to give reassurance. They may also feel it is a way to show the power of their convictions.

Again though, this backfires, as it often results in a shutting down of dialogue - a refusal of politicians to honestly and directly discuss things that haven't gone so well and what can be done to improve them. This closing of dialogue again prevents the public from hearing what really happened or participating in any dialogue to help improve things. We are left frustrated and voiceless.

Using biased language - language or phrasing can be used by politicians to influence how we perceive a particular policy, situation or fact. This can be one of the more subtle forms of political influence that we are subject to, as it can creep into common usage beyond politicians of a particular stripe, and become the common way we perceive an issue, even though it is a biased view.

For example, people's views on the issue of taxation can vary dramatically. Some (generally those on the political left) may see it as a positive thing - an essential way to achieve a better, more cohesive and more equal society by paying for social services and helping to redistribute wealth. Others (towards the political right) may see it as an imposition - where your money is being taken to pay for things you have little control over or may not benefit from. Many people will sit somewhere between these two views.

The language we generally use in the UK to discuss taxation though tends to be drawn from the right wing political view, seeing the 'Taxman' as a faceless bogeyman - someone you're trying to keep your money away from. Advice telling you 'how to beat the taxman' is common, even when it's not politically motivated. Indeed, even the civil service and HMRC have presented it this way! One rarely sees taxation presented in a different way from this in the UK - for example, as a positive thing, which is part of your moral duty to be a good citizen, and where you can make a contribution to a better society in which we're all in it together. And, be aware, this isn't such a ridiculous idea, as it is practiced in other countries, such as Sweden.

The ubiquity of this phrasing and language to discuss something like taxation is not surprising at a time dominated by centre-right politics in the UK - from Margaret Thatcher onwards. It also however shows the lack of an alternative, snappy language from others in society - including those on the political left - to articulate the idea of taxation in a positive way.

It's not just the issue of taxation in which these implicit language biases appear. This point applies to a range of other ideas - for example the idea of 'choice' against the idea of 'regulation'. As we've already noted, we live at a time with a strong neoliberal worldview, which leads to influences that promote the idea of a smaller state and stronger economic markets. This leads to the use of phrases like 'choice' being seen in a positive sense and phrases such as 'regulation' being portrayed as impositions on people's freedom, which drain economic growth and innovation. Under another vision of society though, we could see choice in a different way - as 'waste' or 'greed' or at best pointless past a certain level, as well as seeing regulation in a more positive way - as 'protection', 'social justice', 'fairness' or 'equality'. We could also see the freedoms of the many to live decent lives as being more important than the freedoms of the wealthy few to gain more money and power.

In conclusion, there are several ways of spinning meaning from our language, and the most common uses that influence us can be dependent on the dominant ideas and views overarching our society.

Lying, sowing mistrust, undermining democracy - this section on politics has taken a positive view of the motives of most politicians and people connected to politics, and the influencing methods noted up to here have reflected this. In recent years though, the political game has changed with the rise of the far right in the USA, Brazil and certain countries around Europe.

The tactics used by Trump and other members of the far right have moved beyond the 'normal' (yet still unacceptable) techniques of influence listed so far, and into much more extreme measures, aimed at sowing fear and division between groups in society, undermining confidence in democratic processes and institutions and eroding people's trust in each other and the information they receive.

Our personal reaction to their communications should not just be to exercise 'curious scepticism' but to simply not engage with them. Messages from some sources are just self-evidently untrustworthy, unreliable and not worthy of our attention - and we should treat these as such. We should fight with all our energy against dangerous attempts like this to undermine our democracy and sense of civilisation in society.

ACTION

THINK CRITICALLY ABOUT A POLITICAL MESSAGE

Try this next time you encounter a political message from someone - in any context - whether it's hearing a politician's speech, watching TV news, or hearing someone's opinion on a political issue. Listen to what they say and ask what are the values behind their position? What are they trying to convince you of? What techniques are they (perhaps unwittingly) using to try to convince you? Get into the habit of using this critical thinking to help you develop a clearer picture of where people are really coming from in politics, and who is trying to communicate in the clearest, most honest way.

We have now explored just a few of the techniques people can use to distract from, or put a 'shell of certainty' around, their core arguments. And let's be clear - it's not just politicians that use these techniques. A range of other people and organisations do it, including campaigning groups, television channels and us, when we are seeking to gain power or win arguments rather than entering into proper dialogue to try to understand each other and reach an informed conclusion together.

So, aside from equipping ourselves to navigate political messages better, we should also each try to raise the standard of our political conversations with others. If we don't like being manipulated, why should we do it to other people? Improving our political discussions throughout society - starting with our own - could enable us to actually listen to each other about what we agree and disagree on, have productive conversations and start to build a better world together.

ACTION

PRACTICE GOOD POLITICAL DISCUSSION

Think carefully when you have political conversations with people. Pay them the respect of listening to them carefully, challenge them if you think they're trying lazy tricks to convince you of their views and instead try to get to the essence of their views - which is where the most fulfilling and interesting political conversations happen. Why do they think that refugees should only be able to stay in this country for 5 years? Is that an arbitrary figure? What are their values and beliefs that led them to this view?

And in return, don't use influencing tricks to 'win' arguments, but discuss the values you care about that have led you to adopt your particular view on an issue, and why you've decided to adopt a particular position, even if you do recognise that it might ultimately be arbitrary. This will yield much more nourishing conversations, enable you to adopt better informed views and to refine and adapt these views based on actually being willing to learn from other people's views!

7. MANAGE YOUR THOUGHTS

In this chapter, we have explored some of the benefits and pleasures of thinking and reflecting. But thinking well doesn't mean thinking too much - and it can be harmful to become too attached to our internal world and cling to all the thoughts that pass through our heads.

Learning how to manage our thoughts and our relationship with them is not only an important part of thinking well - it is an essential part of our mental health.

Part of this is to be aware of what our thoughts are - they are inventions of our brain - and although they can make us feel anything from joy to extreme distress, they are things we can choose to ignore or change.

In some forms of mindfulness practice, we are encouraged to see our thoughts as like a flowing river - something rolling past us, that we don't have to jump into. Just because a particular thought is going through our head, it doesn't mean we need to grab it, accept it and let it affect us. We can instead just become aware of our thoughts 'passing by' in our head and note with interest what they contain and how our brain is thinking. This gives us a useful sense of separation from our thoughts, and means that we can then choose which ones to use and accept, rather than feeling overwhelmed and influenced by every thought we have.

Another element of 'thought management' is recognising which thoughts or types of thinking are helpful to us and which aren't. We've already argued that we can separate ourselves from our thoughts and don't have to engage with all of them, so it would seem to make sense to only engage with those that are helpful to us, and ignore or drop those that aren't. When stated like this, it sounds very easy to do but for many of us it is incredibly difficult, and people can be tormented by negative thoughts from self doubt to jealousy.

The first step when we are struggling with this, or any other aspect of our thinking, is to be gentle with ourselves and not burden ourselves with more negative thoughts such as self criticism. Instead we should try to notice the thoughts, how they are making us feel and see if we can make the choice to ignore them, challenge them or think of something more constructive. This approach is similar to some of that used in Cognitive Behavioural Therapy (CBT counselling), and if you are experiencing distress or problems with your thoughts or mental health, you should consult your GP or other trusted healthcare provider.

Our mental health is of course a massively important and complex area, and we would not want to reduce our insights on this to a few paragraphs. These are some general starting points to help you start a better relationship with your thoughts. We will come back to challenging unhelpful thoughts in chapter 9 'How can I get the most out of life?', but if you wish to explore this issue further, you could contact a leading mental health provider like Mind or the Mental Health Foundation. But, to repeat this important point, if you are experiencing distress or problems with your thoughts or mental health, you should consult your GP or other trusted healthcare provider.

PART 3

PLANNING YOUR JOURNEY

CHAPTER 8

HOW SHOULD I RELATE TO OTHERS?

How should I relate to other people? —
How should I treat others?

We live on this planet with billions of other people and creatures. How should we treat, and relate to, these 'others'? This chapter will explore this question, and will try to challenge some of our assumptions about how we think about the other living entities around us.

We will start by exploring the fundamental question of how we should relate to other people in the first place.

Needless to say, this chapter touches on our values, and we'll talk about these more in the following chapter, but this is about more than just values. It's about how you see human life and your connection with other people - and ultimately, all other living things. It's a big question, so let's get started.

HOW SHOULD I RELATE TO OTHER PEOPLE?

Our attitude towards, and bond with, other human beings is influenced by a range of things - from our evolved instincts to the social and cultural influences around us. Some of these factors pull us towards certain people - for example, when we are born one of our first instincts to kick in is to find the nipple of our mother so that we can gain food. Some of these factors however can push us away from other people - such as living in a racially intolerant society.

As a result of these factors, each of us ends up with a particular view of other people and how we should relate to them.

Before we consider how we should relate to, and treat, other people, we should briefly challenge our own assumptions about other people.

It's very easy to generalise about other people in order to justify our existing attitudes or behaviour towards them or towards life - for example, using the idea that 'everyone's just in it for themselves' to justify a more selfish attitude to life. But what are people really like?

WHAT ARE OTHER PEOPLE LIKE?

As we've already noted in this book, it's not possible to look into the minds of other people. This means we spend our adult lives making judgements about their worldviews, thoughts and motivations in order to work out how to interact with them.

We often make these judgements based on our own experiences. This method can sometimes give us a reasonably accurate understanding of how they're seeing things - for example, when it relates to a universal experience - if someone hits their finger with a hammer, we can assume they, like us, will be feeling pain. If we only judge other people's experiences through our own however, this can often lead us to inaccurate judgements about what people are thinking and why they are feeling this way - which can in turn lead us to making inaccurate judgements about them as a person. And when these

143

judgements are negative this can sow division between people - both individuals and groups. For example, someone's experience of life as a white person may well be quite different to those of a black person.

It is therefore important to use empathy in our relations with, and in thinking about, other people. We should put ourselves in their shoes and try to see things from their position, even if we don't have a full picture of their background or the factors that have shaped their worldviews.

When thinking about other people, we suggest it is reasonable to start by assuming they are just like us. And you need to look at yourself honestly in order to see what this really means.

If you're like me, which I assume you are, you have good intentions and want to treat other people well. There are probably some people whose welfare you care about even more than others, such as family and friends, but this doesn't diminish your overall desire to treat others well. Despite your good, universalist intentions though, you also need and want things for yourself - from material goods such as food to social goods such as respect and affection from others. Like mine then, your life is an ongoing act of trying to balance these sometimes competing needs and you may not always get it right. As well as trying to manage these competing and complex needs, you are a creature that is not simply a 'rational calculating machine' - you are prone to particular behaviours, and may also have times where you just aren't in the mood to try to be nice to others.

This is of course a very simplistic portrait of myself - and perhaps of you and other people. But it does perhaps start to shed some light on how we should see others, and how we can set fair and realistic expectations for them.

- The first thing it shows is that other people are trying to navigate a very complex and challenging life as best as they can, just as you are. Realising this is a great starting point in building a sense of understanding with other people.
- They are also probably doing it imperfectly, just as you are. This is another important point of commonality between

people, and suggests we should acknowledge this before judging other people and also before criticising them or their actions.

- Like you, most other people probably also have good intentions at heart. They are sometimes fair and sometimes not, but are trying to navigate life as best they can, just as you are. This suggests we shouldn't live with a constant suspicion of other people's motives, as they're likely to be similar to yours. Adopting this mindset can make us feel much less anxious and 'on guard' and much warmer towards people. And even when people's behaviour or motivations aren't great, we should try to give them the benefit of the doubt if we can, rather than getting on to our moral high horse, as we are prone to just the same moral lapses and moments of selfishness as they are.

There are of course a few people who will not fit into this category, and will want to harm others, and even though there may be reasons for this in their background that are not their fault they still need to be stopped and you need to be on guard against them - but the key thing is that we can assume most people are not like this.

This approach doesn't mean you need to be a pushover. If you know people who consistently behave badly after you've given them the benefit of the doubt a couple of times then you may need to drop a conciliatory approach. But at least you gave them the chance - and this doesn't diminish the value of developing a less suspicious and more empathetic approach to thinking about others and their motives.

Taking a co-operative approach like this to solving conflict, global politics and other areas of human interaction has been shown to be successful by academic experiments, including those on the famous 'Prisoner's Dilemma' by Robert Axelrod, Professor of Political Science and Public Policy at the University of Michigan.[45]

45 heritage.umich.edu/stories/the-prisoners-dilemma/

These simple conclusions can help us to think in a more understanding way about other people, and can help us relate to them better - from giving us a greater sense of connection to others, based on us realising that we are all trying our best to navigate a complex and challenging experience of life, through to giving us better approaches to resolving potential conflicts.

HOW SHOULD I RELATE TO OTHER PEOPLE?

This may seem like a very peculiar question to ask, as the answer seems obvious. The traditional answer would seem to be as follows:

> *Human beings are social creatures, and we need each other. Relationships with other people are what give our lives meaning. We should therefore strive for good, close relationships with as many people as possible. We should not just seek good relationships with our existing friends and family - but with everyone we encounter. Even when we meet people that we disagree with or dislike, this is usually down to some failure of communication, understanding or a lack of moral virtue or enlightenment on our part.*

You may not have seen it articulated in this way before, but this is the all-embracing attitude towards relationships with other people that seems to overarch our modern society.

Whilst this is a well-meaning viewpoint containing some useful principles, it also raises a number of questions. Few would argue that human beings are generally social creatures, but does this really mean that we have a moral obligation to seek the closest possible relationships with all other people?

We shouldn't of course aim to do harm to other people (although this isn't always possible but that's another moral question) and we should aim to be kind and compassionate to all other people. But these are statements of how we should behave towards other people - questions of our moral conduct - which we will deal with in the next chapter.

The issue becomes trickier when we ask what sort of relationships we should have with other people. I would argue that there is a pressure in modern society (as noted in the statement earlier) to be gregarious, make as many friends as possible and get close to as many people as possible. It is seen as the sign not only of a morally worthy person but of someone who has lived a more fulfilled life.

We should challenge this idea, as not only is it an exhausting conception of how we should live our lives, it is completely arbitrary and may not be the way that everyone wants to live.

It may seem a strange and even antisocial thing to suggest, but the reality is that we have a choice in how we engage with other people, as well as whether we engage with them in the first place. We are so immersed in our social habits that we often don't realise we have this choice in our interactions. But maybe we should give it some thought and consider whether this particular approach works for us - or whether another would make our life better?

The simple fact is we don't have to strive to get to know everyone personally and have close relationships with them, even though we are often told that connection with other people is something we need to strive for.

Being liked is seen as an important currency in today's world, and we use the word 'currency' deliberately as this seems like a very capitalist idea of how to behave. The aim seems to be to be as popular as possible, have the biggest social networks possible and ultimately greater influence. This extends from our relationships with people we meet in daily life to the contacts we have with other people online.

But like money, what do we do with this influence if there's nothing we want to spend it on?

Massive numbers of friends are of little use to us if we are spreading ourselves too thinly among them, with not enough time to spend with all of them, and if the relationships aren't particularly strong. Studies suggest that each of us can realistically maintain a social circle of a maximum of 150 people. And why should we even have this many - as who is putting a figure on the number of friends we should have? Also, what if we don't particularly want 'social influence' and feel it is a bit of a shallow idea?

This pursuit of these aims of popularity and influence comes at quite a cost to us - and significantly greater cost for some people. Building relationships takes effort, time and energy and can be hard work, even for people who enjoy doing it. But there are many people for whom the (self-imposed) pressure to build as many relationships as possible and behave in super-social ways brings an enormous amount of stress and anxiety, as they may not be naturally inclined to behave like this.

We are all different in terms of the amount and type of social exposure we want, the relationships we want with others and how much solitude we like. Some of us are more extroverted or introverted than others, and whatever you are is fine! The problem is that these aims that surround us for popularity and super-social behaviour make many people forced into behaviours that aren't really 'them', which brings them stress and misery when trying to follow them, and brings them great suffering when they feel they aren't achieving these ideals.

All of this may seem rather abstract, but these issues affect all of us, and can cause particular anguish for young people in a digital age who are looking to establish their status and sense of self in the world. We need to show them that it's not all about 'likes' or the number of people you know. It's about having the relationship with other people that works for you, and about having quality not quantity of relationships.

So why are we using our personalities to ingratiate ourselves with as many people as possible in order to achieve aims that are arbitrary and don't really matter?

This 'relationship treadmill' feels very similar to the 'work treadmill' we put ourselves on to achieve more and have greater material success by doing jobs we don't really like, in order to achieve aims that we don't really care about (such as earning more money) that are completely arbitrary and have arisen from other influences in society. Let's look at this relationship treadmill now, and try to understand where these assumptions have come from so we can challenge them.

This idea of 'maximising our social influence' partly feels like something that has stemmed from the influence of turbo capitalism in recent decades - the idea that we should be selling our personal 'brand' - that we are actually commodities that we need to sell to other people. This, of course, is nonsense.

There is also the misplaced idea that our popularity (measured by number of friends or acquaintances) is a key way in which we should be judging our self worth. This is a completely arbitrary judgement, and has brought a lot of suffering to many people - from children to teenagers to adults - who feel that they aren't popular enough and therefore don't have any value as people. This is an incredibly powerful influence on us and is hard to challenge, but it is again ultimately arbitrary nonsense, and we do not have to let it dictate how we behave or feel in our lives - we can just ignore it.

We should instead peel back all the layers of nonsense and arbitrary judgements about how our relationships with other people should be, and instead focus on some simple principles that matter about how we should treat other people. For example:

- Be kind and compassionate to other people - try not to harm them
- Respect other people's humanity
- Try to empathise with them before you judge or criticise them
- Give them the benefit of the doubt at least once
- Apply these principles to all other people - treat people equally and don't discriminate

Beyond this though, it should be up to us how we choose to relate to people, with no judgements on ourselves or others on how we or they choose to do this. This isn't about saying we should treat other people with suspicion or coldness, but about realising that we have a choice in how we relate to others.

So, don't judge yourself on the number of friends you have or the influence you feel you possess. None of this matters. Don't feel you have to ingratiate yourself with everyone you meet, make as many friends as possible or even seek close relationships all the time. For example, you can say 'no' when people ask you to meet for a coffee or take other steps to build a relationship with you. You may feel a sudden sense of freedom at being able to have a choice in this!

What matters is treating other people well on a day to day basis and having the range and quality of relationships that suits us as individuals - and this may differ significantly for different people.

You may be someone who is gregarious and loves to be meeting new people all the time and at every social event - and that's great. But you may instead be someone who is more introverted and enjoys their own company - and the important thing is, this is fine too, and you should not be seen as less moral, successful or likeable if you are this way or choose to live your life this way. Don't buy the idea that we have to be all things to everyone. Life your own life and don't judge yourself (or let other people judge you) on arbitrary ideas and dogmas that cause you suffering.

ACTION

HOW DO YOU WANT TO RELATE TO OTHERS?

It may not be something you've considered before, but think about how you like to relate to others. What are your natural preferences in terms of how you relate to others? Do you feel you are on a 'friendship treadmill' in some way? How would you change it to suit your natural preferences more? See if you can set out the ways you'd like to relate to other people in future.

HOW SHOULD I TREAT OTHERS?

Let's move on from how we relate to others to an issue at the centre of our moral choices and conduct - namely, how we treat others. This includes both other human beings and other creatures on this planet.

OTHER HUMAN BEINGS

The one factor that unites us is that we are all human beings, with the same basic genetic makeup and all trying to make the best of their experience of life.

This fact has been the starting point for many of the moral views we have about how to treat others. It leads to the idea that we should treat every person with an equal amount of respect and care, regardless of any other differences between us. This principle has been a leading tenet of modern political democracies and human rights agreements.

It seems a reasonable decision to draw a line around our own species to give it special treatment in how we behave towards other members of it, as although it is an arbitrary line (and moral decision), it is trying to apply fair principles to as many creatures as possible that share our basic traits and concerns.

It may however have influenced (for the worse) how we perceive and treat other creatures beyond human beings - making us feel that they are somehow 'below us' or outside our basic moral obligations. In a moment we will explore this further and argue that the time might be right to extend our 'line of moral concern' to include other creatures than human beings in these principles.

We should also note that human beings sometimes find it hard to apply this moral principle even to all members of their own species. When we discriminate against particular groups of human beings (such as those with a different skin colour to us, or those of a different religion or gender), judging them to be unworthy of the full status or moral obligations we ascribe to others, this is the starting point for some of the most shameful and horrific episodes in human history. There is therefore a strong practical as well as moral argument for equality among human beings.

These thoughts lead to some simple moral principles about how to treat other people, and we have set these out in the previous section, on page 149.

OTHER ANIMALS

The question of how we should treat other creatures is not just a moral one - it has major practical implications across our daily lives and global society, including the food production systems we use, our impact on the environment and whether we are able to feed the planet's population adequately.

Our starting point in thinking about this issue is not practical though - it is to simply remember that we, human beings, are as much a part of the natural world as any other living thing. Despite millennia spent trying to convince ourselves that we are separate from, or somehow above, the natural world, we are part of it.

We all urgently need to realise this, and feel the emotional bond to the rest of nature that we perhaps lose when we have spent so long trying to distance ourselves from it. Many people's lives in the modern world are too distanced from nature, and everyone needs opportunities to renew their bond with it. This will not only improve our well-being, but may also also have the positive effect of making us more inclined to treat it better.

When we see ourselves as part of nature, it feels right and fair to have a harmonious relationship with the rest of it, including not causing unnecessary suffering to other animals.

When we look at our current relationship with nature, it is truly stretching the boundaries of credibility to suggest that we are behaving in a way that is anywhere near consistent with these principles. Just consider the way we currently treat and use other animals. We are extremely inconsistent and morally fuzzy in this. For some animals, such as household pets, we have a massive affection and affinity and are prepared to sacrifice our own comfort and lifestyles for them. But we are willing to treat billions of other creatures as sources of food or as expendable objects that can be terminated or moved on when they are of no use to us or in the way of our ambitions (from birds nesting in our roofs to animals living in rainforest areas that we want to clear). Somehow this just doesn't feel right.

I suggest we should take a further step back and challenge our assumptions about how we currently treat animals in the modern world. We need to apply some clearer and more consistent moral principles. This step is to ask, following our initial discussion of this in a previous section, whether the time might be right to extend our 'line of moral concern' from human beings to include other creatures, and apply the same moral principles to how we treat these creatures as we do to human beings.

Extending these principles (including ascribing rights) to animals may seem like an absurd idea, but it is perhaps more useful to ask why we wouldn't do this. For example, why is it wrong to murder another a human being, yet an integral part of our food production system to murder millions of cows, pigs, chickens and other animals on an industrial scale every day?

There are a range of assumptions behind why we treat animals the way we do in the modern world. Let us outline some of them now, and see if we can challenge them:

Their experiences aren't comparable to human beings - we have the idea that other animals aren't as intelligent as human beings, yet it's quite clear that many suffer and feel pain and fear, just as we do. This seems more than enough reason to apply principles we use for humans (like 'try not to do harm') to animals too. If we're basing our moral radius on their intelligence, this is more complicated than we might think, as there are many species of animal of reasonably high intelligence. This raises the question of what attributes or levels of intelligence should qualify an animal species to be the subject of our respect and compassion? For example, if it's based on intelligence, should dolphins have rights but not horses? It seems much better to put the responsibility for moral principles on us rather than them - as we are the ones that control and adjust our moral principles and other animals can't control what they are. And this means, if we want to see ourselves as moral creatures, we should apply the same basic moral principles we apply to humans (such as 'do no harm') to other creatures too.

They are not human beings - this is the idea that we have drawn our moral line around human beings simply because we are members of the same species, and that we should therefore apply stronger moral principles to our dealings with our own species than others. This would seem to be how we often approach our moral obligations (or lack of them) to other creatures, as we even still conduct horrific experiments on our closest animal relatives, chimps and apes. This view of humans as superior to, and separate from, other animals is still a dominant one in modern culture and emerged from a point in time when we had far less understanding of humans and other animals. It has also been strengthened by lots of religious and other ideological ballast over the years. It doesn't seem unreasonable to put human beings first, but is there not perhaps some moral virtue in giving animals a higher set of rights than we do now, especially as setting these moral boundaries and allocating these rights is an arbitrary thing?

Tradition - I suggest a big reason we still treat animals in this way and maintain this particular moral view is simply because we always have, and many of the cultural and institutional influences around us help to maintain it. For example, although the number of people adopting vegetarian or vegan lifestyles has massively increased in recent years[46], the consumption and promotion of meat and dairy products is still the norm in our schools, shops, restaurants and other

46 The number of U.S. consumers identifying as vegan grew from 1% to 6% between 2014 and 2017, a 600% increase — www.forbes.com/sites/janetforgrieve/2018/11/02/picturing-a-kindler-gentler-world-vegan-month/

areas of our daily lives. So, our adherence to this moral view and lifestyle choice is for reasons of tradition rather than any more convincing moral or practical reasons.

Inertia - for many people it feels inconvenient to change their lifestyles to be consistent with these principles, even though many might acknowledge that the principles are reasonable. But living in a way that's consistent with our values can feel good for us and can lift a burden of guilt off our backs.

In fact, from a practical point of view, it could be argued that there is little reason left to eat animals. We suggest that our view of our relationship with animals and how to treat them is very old-fashioned and out of date - from a time when people sourced their food locally, food supply was more scarce and animal husbandry was needed to supplement our diets.

Now, in the days of global supply chains and advanced food production techniques, all that has changed and we don't need animals for food anymore, as we can gain the nutrients we need from plant-based and other sources. At the same time, the use of animals in these global supply chains leads to greater cruelty and environmental impact than ever before. In fact animal production is preventing us from feeding people around the planet more effectively and with less environmental impact. In short, we have an opportunity to get the best out of food production in the modern world, but we are currently getting the worst out of it. We just need to remove animals from the equation to make it work and take this opportunity.

Ultimately, this is a tricky moral question, and like all other moral questions, the answer is arbitrary. And whilst it's a complex question, it's certainly not an absurd one.

In fact, I suggest we are at a time of human society and technological development where we should reflect on our relationship with other animals and consider whether we want to adjust our arbitrary moral compass a little to give them more rights - as this adjustment would reflect well on us as a species. Indeed, we suggest that in 30 years' time, human beings might look back and ask why on earth we kept eating animals and treating them in this way for so long. The renewal of our bond with nature is perhaps the most urgent task for human beings in the modern world.

ACTION

HOW SHOULD YOU TREAT OTHERS?

Take some time to reflect on the questions raised in this chapter. For example, how should I treat other human beings? And how should I treat other animals beyond human beings? If you reach some conclusions that mean you have to change your behaviour towards others, try to apply these new behaviours from now.

CHAPTER 9

HOW CAN I GET THE MOST OUT OF LIFE?

Appreciate your existence - Savour life — Wonder and curiosity — Set realistic expectations — Know yourself — Be resilient — Work out what you can control — How to be happy — Get into nature — Health

You are unbelievably lucky. Why? Because you exist.

So, what are you going to do with that 80 years of life?

In this chapter we will explore some ideas on how you can make the most of the time you have to exist. We could see this period as a window of opportunity to experience what it's like to be alive. Many of the points we cover are therefore about optimising this experience of life, and keeping ourselves in a state of health that enables us to do this.

These points aren't intended as precepts for living - you should work out your own, based on how you want to use the remainder of your time of being alive. But the following thoughts should provide some initial ideas to get you thinking.

ACTION

HOW DO I WANT TO LIVE?

Before you start thinking about the detail of what you'd like from your life (which we'll do later in this chapter), stand back and look at the bigger picture. What's the overall approach you'd like to take to living? In this book, and the chapter that follows, we've opted for the idea of a considered approach to living, based on the idea that we have only a short, finite life span which we should optimise whilst living within the parameters of the planet and the need to be fair and kind to others. But you may want to take a different approach - for example, just living and seeing where the journey takes you, or living a life of as much pleasure as possible. Have a think about the approach you'd prefer, and before adopting it, think about both its advantages and disadvantages.

APPRECIATE YOUR EXISTENCE

You are alive. Isn't that amazing?

Your atoms have coalesced into a viable living creature, formed on a planet with the highly fortunate placement in its solar system to be able to accommodate life.

Through a lucky draw in the evolutionary lottery, you were born and have survived up to this point where you are now reading this book. What's more, you have been born into a species with the capacity to reflect on your own existence and to appreciate the fact that you are alive – a quality that, as far as we know, other species do not possess.

Somehow, you have emerged temporarily out of the non-experience of not-living, for a brief period of 80 years or so, to be living.

Many of us tend to be so busy and absorbed in the pressure and rush of everyday living that we rarely (if ever) take time to step back from our lives and appreciate the remarkable fact that we are alive and what this really means.

Learning to appreciate life like this, and reminding yourself about it regularly, can be one of the great pleasures of life, and can add a real sense of meaning to your life. No matter how difficult everyday living may be sometimes, seeing our lives in this wider context can help us to put everyday worries into perspective and give us a great sense of calm.

Make sure you take time to regularly reflect about the simple, remarkable fact that you are alive. At the end of each day just register your gratitude and appreciation for this - not necessarily to anyone or anything (like a god) in particular – the important thing is just to acknowledge your luck in existing.

ACTION

START A DAILY GRATITUDE HABIT

At the end of each day before you go to sleep, take a couple of minutes to reflect about the amazing fact you are alive, and feel a sense of gratitude that you exist, regardless of what's happened during the day. This can not only have a positive impact on your well-being but is also a great way to end the day with a sense of clarity and perspective on your life.

REFLECT AND SAVOUR YOUR EXPERIENCES

No matter how busy or intense your life is, you can afford to give yourself some time each day to extract yourself from the rush and find somewhere peaceful to sit quietly without disturbance for at least ten minutes. If you want to, you can use this time to reflect on something, such as your experiences in the day so far or your situation as a small human being in a massive universe. But you could also use this time to not reflect on anything, and instead seek stillness and peace. You could choose to do this in any way you like - from walking in the country to meditating to sitting on a park bench.

Taking this time to stand back and reflect can be fulfilling in itself. It can give us a sense of calm and clearer sense of context on our lives and situations.

We should also remember to savour the experience of being alive, as well as the individual experiences we have as we go through them. This doesn't always mean sitting in a field with our legs crossed though. We can appreciate the busier aspects of life as well as the quieter ones. For example, it can be satisfying to reflect on the enjoyment we are feeling when we are in the middle of busy, social experiences with other people, such as parties. Taking a few seconds to do this occasionally can enable us to 'check in' with ourselves during these experiences and fully appreciate them.

Research has shown that practising awareness of sensations, thoughts and feelings can improve both the knowledge we have about ourselves and our well-being.

SEE THE WORLD WITH A SENSE OF WONDER AND CURIOSITY

The attitude with which you live your life matters. I suggest it pays to approach life with a sense of wonder and curiosity.

It's easy to get bogged down in the details, responsibilities and worries of daily living, but if we can keep in the back of our minds the insight that we are just creatures temporarily living on a planet in a massive universe, this can help us to find little chinks of light in daily life - moments when we allow this wider reality to penetrate our daily routine. These are the moments where we look up to the sky, enjoy the clouds passing by and wonder why the sky is blue, or where we look below the grass to see the tiny ecosystem living there. Moments when we feel a sense of wonder.

There is endless wonder in the commonplace, yet we tend to take many incredible things for granted - for example the fact that there are feathered creatures flying in the air around us, that the sun creates a beautiful orange light when it sets and that we can create books and poems simply from the ideas in our brains.

These, and millions of other incredibly simple things, pass us by most of the time. So try to remind yourself to pause and truly see the world each day.

It is tempting to use the phrase 'child-like' to describe this sense of wonder, but this implies it is a naïve attitude, or one we will grow out of when we have matured. On the contrary – it is one we should seek to maintain throughout our lives, partly for the joy and energy it will bring us, but also because our lives and the universe hold an infinite array of wonders. To quote the great Carl Sagan "Somewhere, something incredible is waiting to be known."

If we tire of discovering these wonders, the argument goes, we tire of life.

The same applies to learning. We should see the whole of our lives as a learning experience – not simply the period in which we are at school. We should be open to learning and absorbing new things throughout life, as even (indeed, especially) the most intelligent and wise people never stop learning.

There are many reasons why we should do this - including giving us greater fulfilment in life, keeping our brains working and possibly offering us the potential for interests, work or other things that we love that could change the direction of our lives.

This doesn't necessarily mean having to take evening classes or learn in a formal sense - but just to be curious about the world around us. One way to do this is again to interrupt the normal routines that we get into in daily life, where we get into a tunnel vision where we only focus on what needs to be done next or the time we have to be somewhere, at the expense of all the other opportunities the world is offering us. It might simply mean interrupting or adapting our habits occasionally to ask things like 'what if I went a bit further up this road to see what was there rather than turning the corner here as I usually do?' or 'that was an unusual bird sound. Why don't I look up what it is?'. These habits of 'bite sized' learning and curiosity can be very rewarding for us.

SET REALISTIC EXPECTATIONS

We could live pretty blissful lives if all that came into our heads were the things we've discussed so far in this chapter - appreciating life and seeing the world with a sense of curiosity and wonder. But, as you know, our worldviews are formed by a great deal more than this.

One of the areas of thought that can profoundly affect how we see the world and live our lives is the expectations we set for ourselves and our lives. Some of these may be subconscious and we may not be aware of them, but it is useful to review and reassess them to ensure we are not setting arbitrary, unrealistic expectations that will cause us pain and disappointment.

ACTION

REVIEW YOUR EXPECTATIONS OF LIFE

Find somewhere quiet and take a few minutes to think about the expectations you've set for yourself in life. Not just the obvious ones - dig a little deeper to see if there are any assumptions you're carrying with you and judgements you're making about yourself in relation to them. Then remind yourself these expectations are arbitrary and ask whether you want to continue carrying them with you.

In a video interview a few years ago discussing the lessons he had learned from life so far, Stephen Fry noted an interesting thought. He suggested: "The worst thing you can do in life is set yourself goals." His point seemed to be this - when you set goals you either fail to meet this arbitrary target and go through the negative experience of feeling you've failed, or you achieve the goal and then say 'now what?' - and realise the futility of the goal itself anyway. You can also end up not being happy with the life you have lived, what you have achieved and the things you do have, if they are different from the goal you set.

Perhaps even worse than this, when we set expectations or goals for ourselves in life (such as 'I'd like to study at Cambridge University'), we can end up tying them to our sense of self-worth. This can be a bad thing to do, as we don't see the value and good in ourselves for who we are, but we make it dependent on achieving (sometimes unrealistic, but always arbitrary) goals. It's fine to be ambitious but don't tie your self image to achieving specific goals, as this makes your view of yourself contingent on achieving these goals, when it should just be positive all the time.

So, before you set any expectations or goals for yourself in life, make yourself a promise - that you will keep your view of yourself and sense of confidence in yourself separate from whether you achieve these goals or not.

And if you're going to goals and expectations for yourself, make them positive and realistic. Then, remind yourself that they are ultimately arbitrary and set by you, so you don't have to tie yourself to them anyway. As an alternative, perhaps you could simply avoid setting goals for yourself.

But either way, our main advice is to simply 'stop chasing'. This is a piece of wisdom that Buddhism teaches - the idea that yearning for things is at the heart of many of our anxieties and problems - and we will lead much happier and more fulfilled lives if we let go from this yearning and simply accept and appreciate the life and things we do have, and just enjoy living.

KNOW YOURSELF - AND BE HAPPY WITH YOURSELF

It's important to develop a strong (but flexible) sense of your own identity, values and beliefs.

Our personal identity is our sense of who we are, what matters to us and how we feel about ourselves. Our ability to build, nurture and protect it has a significant bearing on what we get from our lives and our experience of them.

A strong sense of identity gives you a secure place from which to deal with the world around you – a set of judgements and instincts you can trust in a complex world full of competing pressures and influences. You can also return to this place whenever you like to remind yourself of who you are, what your qualities are and of what makes you happy.

We often develop this sense of identity over time rather than instantly, and it needs to be nurtured and tended. Try to develop an honest sense of what you are really about, including what makes you happy and fulfilled, what makes you unhappy or uncomfortable, what your priorities are in life and how you really want to live. Don't judge yourself on your choices – just be honest with yourself.

Another important element of your identity is learning to be happy with yourself - or at least accepting who you are. This includes accepting our natural tendencies, qualities and physical features and realising that we are neither perfect nor imperfect – we are just ourselves.

It also means being a friend to yourself - seeing the best in yourself and making the best of yourself, rather than attacking yourself with self-doubt and negative thoughts. Trust yourself and be comfortable with your judgements and choices unless you have good reason not to – stay open minded but resist attacks to your identity. This will help you to live on your own terms, rather than feeling you have to follow others. Don't be afraid to be yourself and to let yourself flourish.

BE RESILIENT

Resilience is much more than just a thinking skill - it is a life skill that takes courage and perseverance to develop. Yet it is vital in helping us negotiate the peaks and troughs that we all encounter in life without them completely derailing us.

Here are some basic pointers on how to develop resilience. When you encounter adversity or major challenges, see them in a wider context. Remind yourself that you are not alone in your situation or the goals you are trying to achieve, and that continued effort and a positive attitude will eventually pay off – the adversity you are going through may eventually subside and the efforts that you are putting in will make a difference.

Also, find some sources of support for yourself – when you can, spend time with people who make you feel good about yourself, who understand you and who like and respect what you're about. When you're not with them, draw support from these friendships and the positive sense of self that you get from them.

WORK OUT WHAT YOU CAN CONTROL – AND WHAT YOU CAN'T

A common fallacy in the modern world is the idea that we are in control of our own lives, and that we can bend everything to our will, just by seizing the day and making it happen.

This is of course nonsense. We can't control everything that happens to us. In fact, most of us probably have far less control over our lives than we think. One of the most useful skills in life is to be able to work out what we can and can't control in the world, and to focus on the things we can control. Coming to terms with this and adapting to it can help us lead a less anxious, more fulfilled and productive life.

For example, we're not in control of how we were brought up or treated by our parents, even though this can significantly affect our worldviews and behaviour in later life. So, rather than feel a sense of injustice and anger about how our upbringing has affected us, we should accept it, and seek to make the best of the person we are and the situation we are in.

Our lives are also dictated far more by chance (or 'luck') than we think. Our parents and upbringing is one example of this. Another is the events that happen to us in life. A musician's big break could have been a matter of just being in the right place at the right time, where a music mogul happened to be in the audience for their pub gig because they were just visiting the area. Equally, another person's tragic accident could have been prevented by them being on the pavement a few seconds earlier or later than when the car skidded out of control and hit them. Often the events we encounter are not as dramatic as these extremes, but things happen to us all the time in life, without our control.

One thing we are more in control of (although not completely, and not all the time) is how we react to the things that happen to us. This includes whether we are willing or able to take opportunities when they arise, and how well we deal with negative or disappointing events and move on from them.

We all go through good and bad times, but we may react to these situations quite differently, depending on who we are, how we're feeling and the context of the event. If we can achieve a balanced, clear-minded reaction to these situations we are more likely to make the best out of them.

Ultimately, this is about knowing ourselves better – knowing our personal histories, preferences and tendencies, and using this understanding to balance how we interpret or respond to particular situations. For example, I know I have a tendency to worry, and imagine that the worst will happen in a given situation. I accept this tendency is out of my control to a certain extent, so when I face a difficult situation (for example, a project has gone wrong at work), I firstly try to acknowledge that I'm likely to imagine the worst-case scenarios. I then remember to calm myself down and take a more relaxed, realistic perspective, and this helps me both stay less anxious and make better decisions.

Another thing we can control is how we equip ourselves to deal with and think about life. By taking the more self-aware and well-informed approach to life that we are advocating in this book, you increase your chances of dealing better with the things you can control, and responding better to the things you can't.

A final area of life to discuss here that we can control is how we assess risk. As we go through life, we make regular decisions about the risks we are prepared to take – from whether to buy that washing machine even though we've not read a review of it, to whether to dive into a river from a steep bank. Each of us differs in the level of risk we are prepared to tolerate, and the threshold of risk we are willing to set. Some of us are daredevils who want thrills whereas others want a more comfortable life where risk is minimised as much as possible.

Where you sit on this spectrum of risk taking is your choice, but it makes sense to get as good as you can be at assessing the risks in life and their associative benefits and weighing them up. You'll need to work out for yourself what an acceptable threshold of risk is in your life. Again, a good dose of self-awareness can help you here, as it could encourage non-risk takers to recognise their tendency for safety, and be a little braver with their decisions and see what benefits they gain from this. On the other side of the coin, it could help risk takers pause and consider before they make decisions or take actions where the risk is ultimately not worth the reward.

LIVE YOUR OWN LIFE

Much of our daily lives as children and adults are spent fending off the influences and ideas of other people as to how we should live.

One of the core elements to a fulfilled life is to be able to carve out the life you genuinely want, and then live happily in this way, without worrying about what other people are doing.

This book has aimed to give you some of the tools and ideas to carve out an independent and well-informed life like this, and in this section we can list a few other ideas to consider when trying to live life for yourself:

Don't compare yourself with other people - as noted in an earlier chapter, human beings have a tendency to make relative rather than absolute judgements, so we are prone to comparing ourselves with others. This can be very unhelpful for our fulfilment and sense of self though, as we may be judging ourselves against an unrealistic or limited view of other people's lives, and constant comparison with other people's lives and experiences can lead us into not paying enough attention to our own. This can lead to our own experiences feeling quite dull, and to us ignoring the true richness and pleasure of our own experiences and lives. And let's remember that our own experiences are the only ones we'll ever have - so we might as well just focus on these and make the most of them!

Live at your own pace - modern life takes place at a frenetic pace. We are surrounded by influences – including the media, employers and even friends - telling us to go faster, take more action and be more productive with our time. It is easy to be swept along by this culture of speed and productivity, and easy to lose sight of the fact that each of us actually has a choice as to the pace of life we adopt.

Some people may enjoy busy, frantic and pressurised lives, but many other people find this way of living extremely stressful, and won't want to reach the end of their lives wishing they'd taken more time to 'enjoy the journey'.

Challenge the modern 'culture of speed', so that you can make an informed choice as to which pace of life suits you best. Here are a couple of ways you can do this.

First, realise you have a choice. Ignore the influences from friends, the media and wider society telling you how you should run your relationship with time. It is up to you, and the first thing to do is realise this and take control of this relationship.

Second, give people more time. Our relationships with other people are some of the most important things in our lives. Allow yourself the time to chat with your neighbours, call your family or stay on the phone a bit longer with your friends.

HOW CAN I BE HAPPY?

People spend a huge amount of time, thought, money and energy on seeking happiness. But what is it that they're actually seeking?

In recent years, happiness has become a serious topic of scientific investigation, and the results of this research to date provide some interesting ideas on how we can improve our mental health and experience of life.

It's actually very difficult to define exactly what we mean by 'happiness'. A useful definition comes from Action for Happiness, a charity that uses the latest scientific evidence to seek happier lives for people - "Happiness is about our lives as a whole: it includes the fluctuating feelings we experience everyday but also our overall satisfaction with life. It is influenced by our genes, upbringing and our external circumstances - such as our health, our work and our financial situation. But crucially it is also heavily influenced by our choices - our inner attitudes, how we approach our relationships, our personal values and our sense of purpose."[47]

Buddhist teacher and author Matthieu Ricard was labelled 'the world's happiest man' after scientists studied his brain. Although he resists this label, his definition of happiness is helpful - he sees it as a sense of 'flourishing' which is experienced deeply, rather than a transient and pleasurable feeling. In this sense, happiness can pervade all we do, regardless of what we do and what we have to do.

At its simplest level we could see happiness as 'how we feel about our lives'. This makes it less a thing that we need to seek and find through external situations and objects, and more something that's accessible through the way we think and perceive our situation.

Before we move on to explore how we can experience more happiness, let us set our expectations realistically, as this is a first step to averting unnecessary misery and anxiety.

---

47 www.actionforhappiness.org/why-happiness

The ideal of perfect happiness is an illusion that the self-help industry has become rich on. And not just the self-help industry, as the illusion of happiness is what many advertisers are presenting in order to convince you to buy their products. But why would we want life to be a period of constant, never-ending happiness anyway? A life like this could be bland, with no variation in our mental state.

To see this, you can try a classic thought experiment. Imagine you could take a 'happiness pill' that would make you happy all the time. Would you want to be in this state for your whole life? Many people would not, and the dystopian consequences of this state have been illustrated by a number of writers, including Aldous Huxley in his 1932 novel Brave New World, in which he portrays a society in which people are rendered docile by happiness, through a happiness pill called 'Soma'.

Perhaps the ups and downs of life give us meaning and colour, as we move between the peaks and troughs and the bits in between, and reflect upon how we feel in these different states.

The fact is that, for most people, life is filled with ups and downs, and feelings other than happiness are perfectly normal facts of the human experience. We all have difficulties in our lives and, as we'll see, one of the ingredients to greater happiness is developing the resilience to deal with them.

So how can we make ourselves happier? According to psychologist Richard Wiseman, "the bad news is that research shows that about 50 percent of your overall sense of happiness is genetically determined, and so it cannot be altered. The better news is that another 10 percent is due to general circumstances (educational level, income and whether you are married or single, etc.) that are difficult to change. However, the best news is that the remaining 40 per cent is derived from your day-to-day behaviour, and the way in which you think about yourself and others."[48]

So, there are plenty of things we can do to push the happiness dial up within this 40% of the total, which could significantly increase the level of happiness we experience in our lives.

48 Wiseman, Richard - 59 Seconds, Macmillan, London 2009, p.11

Here are 10 key steps we can take to achieve this, reproduced here with the kind permission of Action for Happiness[49]. These are based on an extensive review of the latest research evidence relating to psychological/mental wellbeing. As you'll see, some of them reflect points that we have covered elsewhere in this book, but it's good to be able to bring these key influencers of happiness together into a simple list.

1. GIVING

Caring about others is fundamental to our happiness. Helping other people is not only good for them and a great thing to do, it also makes us happier and healthier too. Giving also creates stronger connections between people and helps to build a happier society for everyone. And it's not all about money - we can also give our time, ideas and energy. So if you want to feel good, do good!

2. RELATING

Relationships are the most important overall contributor to happiness. People with strong and broad social relationships are happier, healthier and live longer. Close relationships with family and friends provide love, meaning, support and increase our feelings of self worth. Broader networks bring a sense of belonging. So taking action to strengthen our relationships and create new connections is essential for happiness.

3. EXERCISING

Our body and our mind are connected. Being active makes us happier as well as being good for our physical health. It instantly improves our mood and can even lift us out of a depression. We don't all need to run marathons - there are simple things we can all do to be more active each day. We can also boost our

49 www.actionforhappiness.org/10-keys

well-being by unplugging from technology, getting outside and making sure we get enough sleep!

4. AWARENESS

Ever felt there must be more to life? Well, there is - and it's right here in front of us. We just need to stop and take notice. Learning to be more mindful and aware can do wonders for our well-being in all areas of life - like our walk to work, the way we eat or our relationships. It helps us get in tune with our feelings and stops us dwelling on the past or worrying about the future - so we get more out of the day-to-day.

5. TRYING OUT

Learning affects our well-being in lots of positive ways. It exposes us to new ideas and helps us stay curious and engaged. It also gives us a sense of accomplishment and helps boost our self-confidence and resilience. There are many ways to learn new things - not just through formal qualifications. We can share a skill with friends, join a club, learn to sing, play a new sport and so much more.

6. DIRECTION

Feeling good about the future is important for our happiness. We all need goals to motivate us and these need to be challenging enough to excite us, but also achievable. If we try to attempt the impossible this brings unnecessary stress. Choosing ambitious but realistic goals gives our lives direction and brings a sense of accomplishment and satisfaction when we achieve them.

7. RESILIENCE

All of us have times of stress, loss, failure or trauma in our lives. But how we respond to these has a big impact on our well-being. We often cannot choose what happens to us, but we can choose our own attitude to what happens. In practice it's not always easy, but one of the most exciting findings from recent research is that resilience, like many other life skills, can be learned.

8. EMOTIONS

Positive emotions - like joy, gratitude, contentment, inspiration, and pride - are not just great at the time. Recent research shows that regularly experiencing them creates an 'upward spiral', helping to build our resources. So although we need to be realistic about life's ups and downs, it helps to focus on the good aspects of any situation - the glass half full rather than the glass half empty.

9. ACCEPTANCE

No-one's perfect. But so often we compare our insides to other people's outsides. Dwelling on our flaws - what we're not rather than what we've got - makes it much harder to be happy. Learning to accept ourselves, warts and all, and being kinder to ourselves when things go wrong, increases our enjoyment of life, our resilience and our well-being. It also helps us accept others as they are.

10. MEANING

People who have meaning and purpose in their lives are happier, feel more in control and get more out of what they do. They also experience less stress, anxiety and depression. But where do we find 'meaning and purpose'? It might be our religious faith, being a parent or doing a job that makes a difference. The answers vary for each of us but they all involve being connected to something bigger than ourselves.

WHEN DO YOU FEEL HAPPY?

You can start by simply reflecting on some of the things that make you happy. Be honest with yourself - and select the things that genuinely give you happiness, rather than those you think should. Then, try a different approach. Think back to some times recently when you have felt happy, and reflect on the situation you were in or how you were thinking about life. Were there any common threads that bind these experiences together that enhanced your feelings of happiness? Are you living in a way that provides these things that make you happy? Set out a plan of how you can build more of them into your life.

In summary, if we can develop for ourselves a realistic idea of what happiness actually is, we can, to a degree, take action to improve the amount of happiness we experience.

If we take just a few simple steps to adjust our usual daily routines and our habits of thinking, we can access a happier life without necessarily spending more, consuming more or reducing the happiness of others. Indeed, as we've seen, happiness is not just achieved through meeting our own needs - some of the key ways towards it are through helping, and connecting to, others

GET OUT INTO NATURE

Being around nature can be one of the great pleasures in life, and provides us with a range of benefits for our well-being, whether you are sitting on a bench in your local park or climbing a mountain.

In nature one finds a sense of peace and perspective away from the noise and clutter of modern life. It can act as a balm for our anxieties and can help us see things clearly. We can also get simple pleasure from appreciating the natural beauty and wonder of the world around us.

So, make sure you get out into nature regularly!

LOOK AFTER YOUR HEALTH

As with happiness, life is not perfect and most of us will face some health problems - mental or physical or both - during our lifetimes, and sometimes for their entirety. During these times we need to show resilience as best we can and adapt to the parameters we find ourselves living in. This may sound a little harsh and direct, but it's what we need to do, and is one of the things human beings are good at as a species.

There are however some things that we can control in relation to our health - and these relate to how we look after ourselves - from what we eat to the lifestyles we lead. These steps can help us have a better experience of life with less physical and mental pain (assuming that less pain contributes to a better experience of life). We will briefly explore both the physical and mental sides of our health below.

PHYSICAL HEALTH

In the modern world it is easy to fall into the trap of a sedentary and unhealthy lifestyle – this might be due to the pace and pressure of modern life or the comforts and conveniences provided by modern technology – from televisions to microwaves.

A healthy physical lifestyle – including healthy eating and regular exercise - is however a vital component of our well-being. We just have to look at the benefits of exercise to illustrate this.

Regular exercise is not only good for our physical health – it is also great for our minds. It's amazing how much difference regular exercise can make to your thinking. It can not only make you feel happier and more positive but also more alert and able to think better. You can do it on your own or use it as another way of connecting with people – joining a local sport club or exercise group can not only make you more motivated to do exercise but can also put you in touch with lots of other people with similar interests.

The food we choose to eat is another key thing that shapes our lives, health and happiness. It is also responsible for many of our impacts on the wider world as individuals, including those on the environment and on other people.

In theory it is relatively clear which foods we should be eating (and what we should be avoiding) in order to maintain our physical health. At the same time, however, we live in a complex world with a wide range of choices of what we can eat, and where the facts about food can become obscured by the people and companies looking to make money from our food consumption. It can therefore be easy to lose sight of what we should be eating.

And this matters now more than ever. More than half the UK population is overweight or obese.[50] Globally, things are getting steadily worse - according to the World Health Organisation (WHO), obesity more than doubled between 1980 and 2014 and overweight and obesity are now linked to more deaths worldwide than underweight.

So, we need to take control of our relationship with food, including understanding what we need to eat to be healthy, and how to maintain good food and exercise habits. There is not enough space in this book to set this out in detail, so read the Life Squared publication 'How to eat and exercise well' for more information on this important topic. It cuts through all the confusion about food and health and makes it as simple as possible to achieve a healthy lifestyle - whilst looking after the planet and saving money.

50 www.nhs.uk/Livewell/Goodfood/Pages/eat-less.aspx

TRY THE LIFE SQUARED EATING PLAN

Live your normal lifestyle for a week, and complete a 'health, happiness spending and impact' diary while you do this. Here's how. Throughout each day keep a note of what you're eating, spending, consuming (in terms of environmental impact - including food miles, production and packaging) and the exercise you're taking. Then at the end of each day note how you're feeling. Good? Bad? Energised? Tired? Stressed?

During this same week, read the free Life Squared publication 'How to eat and exercise well'[51] - simply search for this online. This contains 10 recommendations on how to improve your eating and exercise. Then in the following week, try out all 10 recommendations and keep the same diary as in the first week.

Then at the end of the 2 weeks, compare the two diaries - across each of the different areas - from spending to happiness. Are there any differences? Is it working for you? Hopefully you will see some significant benefits!

MENTAL HEALTH

Approximately 1 in 4 people in the UK will experience a mental health problem each year.[52] Many of us experience mental health issues during, or throughout, our lives and it's something that, in many cases, can be treated - like physical health. Mental health problems often go untreated though, in part because they can be harder to self-diagnose than physical ones though, as it may be obvious that we're suffering from physical pain but we can end up trying to live with, or adjust to, all sorts of mental

---

51 Docwra, Richard - How to Eat and Exercise Well, Life Squared 2017
52 www.mind.org.uk/information-support/types-of-mental-health-problems/
    statistics-and-facts-about-mental-health/how-common-are-mental-health-
    problems/#one

health issues because we can't specify exactly what they are or aren't sure that they're 'real' issues.

We urgently need to change this, and give our mental health the attention it deserves, as it influences our entire worldview and experience of life as individuals. So, our core advice in this section is talk to a GP if you're having any problems or worries at all about your mental health. And, by 'problems or worries', we don't mean something you have to specifically diagnose or something that has got so bad that you're in serious distress. We mean whenever your mental outlook isn't how you think it should be or when you're feeling troubled, anxious or are suffering in some way.

There are several steps you can take to look after your mental health - see the earlier list from Action for Happiness for a good starting point. Here are a few other suggestions:

- **Talk about your feelings** - talking about your feelings can help you stay in good mental health and deal with times when you feel troubled.
- **Eat and drink well** - a healthy diet can play a big role in your mental health, so make sure you eat well. Also, steer clear from things that can negatively affect your health and mood, such as alcohol.
- **Keep in touch** - it's not always easy to see people face to face so make an effort to regularly keep up with people who make you feel good - whether on email, phone or online.
- **Ask for help** - don't suffer in silence. Reaching out to other people and asking for help can make a huge difference when we're finding life difficult. You could speak to family and friends, local support groups or mental health charities. But don't be afraid to admit you're struggling or to call on people's help - you would be keen to do the same for them.

WORK

Over the years, human beings have separated their lives into different sections - 'work' and 'leisure'.

Work can mean different things to different people. Looking back thousands of years, we could see 'work' as the activities people did to hunt and gather food and essential goods to enable their families to survive. But people at that time wouldn't have called this 'work' - they'd have simply seen it as 'life'.

In the past centuries, work has become traditionally viewed as the activities you undertake in order to earn money. It has been shaped by religious and economic ideas, and now carries with it a great deal of baggage, such as the capitalist urge to be as productive and efficient as possible with our time, which could be one of the contributors to our rushed and stressed modern lifestyles. This definition brings other problems too - including making work something of a drudge - something to get out of the way in order to put food on the table, and that is what it remains for many people. This money-led definition also leads us to devalue lots of other important productive activities that contribute to society that are unpaid - from parenting to other forms of caring.

For many people however work is about much more than just making money. It is also a source of purpose in their lives, of achieving something useful, being productive and meeting other people. In short, a way of making good use of their time.

We therefore suggest that, living a well-informed and fulfilled life involves challenging the modern idea of work and all the baggage it carries with it, including the idea of the 8-hour day, the 5-day week, the activities that constitute 'work' and the very idea of 'work' itself.

Why does work have to be separate from leisure? We each have an opportunity to find a balance of activities in our lives that enable us to provide the resources we and our loved ones need, whilst doing the other creative, productive and rewarding activities we want to do, as well as finding ample time for rest and relaxation. We shouldn't seek the dreaded 'work/life balance' - we should simply seek life balance.

This doesn't, of course, mean we're being lazy (to quote a typical judgement of people who challenge the traditional values of work) - it means we're taking control of our lives.

ACTION

THINK ABOUT THE LIFE BALANCE YOU WANT

What do you want to do with your life and time? What are the activities that give you purpose and fulfilment? How can you earn a living from some of them? Try to create a picture of the life you'd like to lead and explore how you could lead it. Go with the 5 day week 9-5 if it suits you but if not, open up your mind and challenge the traditional ideas and assumptions of work to create a life balance that suits you.

CONCLUSIONS

In this chapter we have explored a wide range of ways in which you can make the most of the time you have to exist. This is a non-exhaustive set of ideas but each could make a significant contribution to your experience of life.

ACTION

PULL IT ALL TOGETHER

Take some time out to think about how you can improve your experience of life. Think about how you live now and if there are any steps you can take to make your experience better, given that you only have a finite time on the planet. If it's useful, use some of the ideas in this chapter to inform your thinking.

CHAPTER 10

HOW SHOULD I BEHAVE?

What is morality? — What are values? — Are human beings moral? — What are your values? — Being good — Living in line with your values — Conflicting values — A good society

A central question that occupies many people throughout their lives is how they should behave - both as an individual or as a member of a wider society.

This question opens up the fascinating topic of morality, which we will explore in this chapter. We will explore how we can live good, moral lives, as well as how we can overcome the many challenges in front of us when we try to consistently do the right thing in our lives.

But before we consider how we can be good, we need to explore what it actually means to be good. Let us begin by tackling what we mean by 'morality', 'ethics', "values' and the other rather grey and abstract concepts we talk about in relation to being good. We'll then briefly explore other big questions like whether human beings are actually moral creatures, and what values we have.

WHAT IS MORALITY?

Morality is a human invention. The idea of morality itself is simply an abstract concept that we have made up - just like the ideas of 'good', 'bad' and any other moral labels we apply. This may seem like a controversial statement, but this is because we are so used to being told that these ideas are somehow absolutes, or have been imposed on us from on high by a god or external force. They are not and have not.

And as we will see, the 'made up' nature of morality as an idea does not mean that it is meaningless, relative, or that we can just behave as we like. This is because we care about things. We are social creatures with particular senses, instincts, needs and ideas, so certain things matter to us - for example, protecting our children, avoiding pain and trying to set up rules and arrangements with other people to ensure we won't harm each other.

So, the content of morality matters, even if the label itself (and all the other labels related to it) is made up. Indeed, if we eventually get the opportunity to look back at the end of our lives, an important factor in whether we judge them to have been fulfilling or not may be whether we feel we were able to identify our real values and live in a way that was consistent with them.

What's important about morality is what it stands for. It is an attempt to judge how we should each think and behave while we are alive - towards other people, ourselves, other creatures and the wider world. We could see it as our personal contract with the world. Our values (also an abstract concept we've made up) are our judgements about how we should - or shouldn't - behave.

Because it is an abstract concept, morality can be hard to get a grip on sometimes, as it doesn't consist of clear boundaries between 'right' and 'wrong' - it is a collection of grey areas - questions of degree, and therefore, by its nature, there will be things that people don't agree on. For example, if you agree that women should be able to seek abortions, what is the latest point into the pregnancy you think they should be able to do this? 3 months? 6 months? And why have you drawn your line at this particular point? Notice that you have drawn your line at an arbitrary point for an arbitrary reason, as has anyone else who has an opinion on this matter. This is how morality works.

It is incredibly useful to see morality in this light, as it gives us a more realistic view of how moral language and arguments work, and a more reasonable expectation of what we can expect from our own moral behaviour and values when we start to consider them.

WHAT ARE VALUES?

Values are abstract concepts that we use to guide us as to how to behave. They make judgements about what we should do and what we shouldn't. Values can arise for different reasons.

Our values, or sense of morality or 'how we should behave' are informed by a range of factors. These include:

- **Instincts** - our sense of morality is partly informed by certain natural instincts we have and may have emerged as a result of our biological makeup - for example, the desire to survive or to protect our children and close family. Some recent research suggests we have an empathic bias - "an evolutionary tendency to help those with whom we share the most genes ; i.e. our primary group."[53] This would include family, friends and the people closest to us. Beyond this we have to rely on rationality to help us expand our 'radius of moral concern'.
- **Rational aims** - other aspects of morality have perhaps emerged as a result of trying to achieve particular practical goals - for example, having environmental values so that we don't live in a degraded world, or setting up an informal 'social contract' as a society so that people have some basic rules as to how to treat each other (such as goodwill and

53   Gibbs, John C - Moral development, OUP New York 2014, p.119

social responsibility) to enable us to live alongside each other harmoniously.

• **Influences** - further ideas of how we should behave might have been made up to support religious ideas, maintain power or support prejudices.

Our judgements about what we should or should not do could therefore have arisen for various reasons. We may feel strongly about some of these judgements (for example, a desire to protect our children) but it is also quite possible for other people to indoctrinate us with values that we don't genuinely believe in.

We therefore need to be careful about the values we choose to adopt. We each need to think for ourselves about our values, and try to identify those that we genuinely feel rather than those that others might be trying to instil in us. Follow your values rather than basing them on deference to authority - of any kind.

ARE HUMAN BEINGS MORAL?

Another important insight that the abstract nature of morality gives us is understanding why it is sometimes hard for us to consistently meet some of the moral standards we set ourselves. This is because these standards are not only arbitrary and made up, but are also sometimes inconsistent with our natural inclinations. We can override some of these instincts with rational thinking and determination, but this is not always possible and nor should we expect it to be so.

This doesn't mean that human beings are intrinsically 'bad' or 'sinful' as some thinkers and institutions would have you believe. But nor are we intrinsically 'good'. Instead, we are social creatures that generally see the benefits of cooperation, both for rational and instinctive reasons, and want to put standards and systems in place to achieve this. Some of our natural behaviour is consistent with these moral standards and systems (e.g. caring for our family) but some of it (such as self interest and aggression) can conflict with them. See chapter 3 - 'What am I?' - for more on our tendencies in thinking and behaviour as human beings, and how these can affect our moral outlook and behaviour.

In reality, morality is therefore an ongoing and uneasy balancing act in both our individual lives and wider society - between our instincts and rationality. Our moral expectations, as well as our lives, relationships and moral and political discourse in general could all be improved if we started to recognise this.

We're capable of good or bad, and the conditions in the environment and society around us - from our education to our relationships and economic situation - can have a significant influence on how we behave. Our task is therefore to build a society where the conditions are created to promote 'good' behaviour.

WHAT ARE YOUR VALUES?

So, how can we work out what our own values are?

In the modern world it can be a lot harder than it looks to identify what your values are, as there are many powerful influences trying to persuade you that their values are best, which can cloud your own vision of what really matters.

As already mentioned, we're just animals, possessing certain instincts and prone to certain patterns and responses in our thinking. Both of these can be exploited by unscrupulous people who understand how to manipulate them. For example, our tendency to be influenced by the behaviour and attitudes of large groups of people can lead us to supporting or condoning values that we might otherwise reject - such as the sexist or unequal treatment of women in a male-dominated workplace.

The solution is firstly to clear away the 'fog' of these pressures and influences by learning how to think well (see chapter 7), including exercising critical thinking. We should then take some time to stand back from the world and think about what our values actually are.

CONSIDER YOUR VALUES

Simply take an hour or two to step back and think about what your values are. What are the things you really care about? How should people treat each other and the world around them? Try and come up with a few principles that summarise how you want to try to live your life.

This process doesn't have to be a big intellectual struggle - your values may well be a mixture of instinctive and rational ideas. Some of these will be values you aspire to, even if you don't feel you consistently match up to them yet in your life - for example, being open to helping anyone you see in need.

Other values may simply be instinctive reactions and feelings (e.g. a desire to ensure animals are protected) rather than carefully thought-out rational principles. Be careful though to check that these feelings aren't purely driven out of fear, anger, suspicion or other emotions that are less helpful in enabling us to rise to the values we aspire to.

But don't be put off if your instinctive values feel like the opposite of many of the accepted ideas of what is good and admirable today, as some of these accepted ideas (for example, the idea that we need to be aggressive and competitive to succeed in life) may actually be inconsistent with human flourishing. The point is to identify what really matters to you and to not be ashamed of it.

We should provide a caveat here that while it's important to be strong about your values (a point we'll explore further shortly), it's also important to be open to reason and reflection too. We should be prepared to review and adjust our principles in the light of better evidence or arguments. This doesn't mean you are betraying your beliefs - it means they are evolving and becoming more refined.

To go through a more detailed process of reviewing your values and building your own action plan to live more ethically, read our publication 'How to live ethically'.

BEING GOOD

Just like finding the things that give our lives meaning, our values are subjective to some extent, so you have to reach your own view of what yours are. In this section however we've set out some common values held by many people and thinkers that you may feel you hold as well. All of them contribute towards the overall aim of seeking a fair and just society - with basic principles to help us coexist peacefully.

These principles together could be said to form the Golden Rule - 'treat others in the way you wish to be treated'. This principle has formed a surprisingly common spine through both Eastern and Western traditions of thought, espoused by figures as diverse as Confucius, Jesus and Immanuel Kant.

Indeed, one of the most positive points we can identify in human beings is how, despite all the bad things that we see in the news, we have somehow managed to build societies and rules that enable billions of us to function together in a broadly harmonious way. There may be people who behave badly and we may disagree on certain values, but there is nevertheless a shared sense of some basic moral principles, as well as a sufficient commitment to behaving in line with these principles that keeps us rolling along together.

The values noted below are just an initial, non-exhaustive list to give some examples, and to show how you can start putting these values (and any others you may have) into practice in your daily life:

- **Treat others with kindness** - it could be argued that kindness is one of the most important moral principles there is, as it is done for its own sake and expects nothing in return. It can also make us feel good about ourselves. Showing people kindness and compassion in simple daily behaviour could include smiling at others, reaching out to people and seeing what you can do to make the world better.

- **Show empathy** - think about your effects on others and the outside world.
- **Live peacefully** - seek peaceful coexistence with people. This doesn't mean you have to be a pushover - just seek peace where possible and be willing to be the one taking the extra step to do it – but not such a level of risk as to have completely undermined your own position. For example, pausing before you decide to shout back at someone who has insulted you, and considering whether there is a better way to handle it.
- **Help others** - approach life with the desire to help and be 'of service' to other people. Look beyond yourself and your own interests. For example, give time to people in need when you see them - from visiting an isolated elderly neighbour to volunteering for a good cause.
- **Be just and fair** - live with a sense that everyone should be treated equally and fairly, with the same rules applied to all and reasonable, consistently-applied consequences for those who don't follow them. On a day-to-day level, this could include behaviour such as paying your taxes in full, not demanding special treatment above others and being honest with people. It could also mean seeing every human being as equal, and treating everyone with equal respect and compassion.
- **Share resources fairly** - this point is part of 'fairness' above but is so fundamental we are listing it alone. It is the principle that everyone should have access to food, water, shelter and the other resources essential to a reasonable human life, such as access to education and health care. This could bring some interesting moral challenges for our personal behaviour, such as only taking the basic resources we need, sharing any excess resources we have (including income) and having a principle to never exploit other people.
- **Protect the natural world** - concern and respect for the natural world has been an important human value for thousands of years, but we live in a time where this principle is particularly important - not just as a means to an end (such

as ensuring good lives for future generations) but as an end in itself (to protect the natural world for its own sake).

HOW CAN I LIVE IN LINE WITH MY VALUES?

Possessing a set of values isn't of any use unless you stand up for them and act in line with them in a reasonably consistent way.

But one point that you might have already noticed from your own experience is how hard it can be to live perfectly in line with your values – for example, how to behave in a way that is completely consistent with your environmental values. Would you have to stop consuming anything and only eat windfall apples?

This is a problem that can make life difficult for values-conscious people all the time and cause them a lot of guilt and confusion - how do you try to live in line with your values whilst not feeling guilty that you're not doing enough?

The important point is that, once you've identified your values, working out how to put them into practice can be tricky. Values don't come with a user manual or a clear set of rules to tell us how to put them into practice. For example, there could be a limitless range of actions we could take to live in line with the value of 'caring about other people' - from being kind to strangers to giving more time to our families through to giving 50 percent of our income to people living in poverty.

The list of actions that you need to take to live consistently with each value can therefore be never ending. In addition to this, the actions you need to take can be constantly changing – according to the situation and environment you are in – for example, the advent of a new piece of technology may require you to take new actions to behave in line with your environmental values.

Additionally, even when you do select some actions that could be consistent with your values, there are no rules on where the line should be drawn on the strength of each of these actions. For example, how do we know that giving 50 percent of our income to people living in poverty is consistent with our value of caring about other people? Should it be 70 per cent? Or would 20 per cent be acceptable? Again, there are no rules for this.

In conclusion, there is no simple rule that can tell you how you should live in line with your values. There is no definitive list of actions to take or clear place at which to 'draw the line' for each action. You can learn about what scholars and religions have said about how to live in line with your values, and you can do some research and reflect on it yourself, but ultimately everyone (including religions and scholars) is making up the list of actions they take as well as where they draw their 'line' on each of them, so you will need to do the same.

It can be useful to set some basic rules for yourself for each of your values, as this can make it easier to decide on specific actions to take, and also make it easier to see if you're living in line with your values. For example, for your value of caring for the environment you may decide to make the rule that you want to live your life within your share of the resources of one planet – rather than the equivalent of three planets resources that most of us currently live within. Or for your value of caring for animals, you may decide you're not going to eat or buy any animal products.

You may decide to set completely different rules to these – the point is, if you can, set some rules for how you'll live by each value. This may not be as hard to do as you might think. When you think about your values, you may start to come up with these rules – for example, in your value of caring for the environment you may come up with principles such as 'I want to live within my share of the resources of one planet' or 'I will avoid doing things that harm the environment'.

There are some other conclusions we can draw from the discussion above. First, it shows the importance of thinking for yourself about values, and realising that these judgements are up to you. When anyone tells you something is right or wrong, you should not take their word for it but make your own decision.

Second, it shows that 'the right and the wrong things to do' aren't always as black or white as many people believe – there are often many different ways in which we could live in line with each of our values and in which the line could be drawn within each action. Deciding on how best to put our values into action often has to be a process of weighing up the different possibilities to reach the best set of actions you can, and reviewing this regularly in response to changing circumstances. At asocietal level, this process of balancing the different arguments as to how we should live is one of the aims of the democratic political process.

Thirdly, and most relevant to this section, the discussion above shows why values can be such slippery things to live with – they often don't give us clear guidance or answers on the actions we need to take. We have to work this out for ourselves.

Here are some more general principles to help you live in line with any values you have:

- **Make some simple rules** - establish a few simple, memorable principles of how to live (e.g. 'Be kind to everyone'). Having these in your mind can really help you to make better decisions and do so quickly.
- **Identify some priorities** - set out some basic actions you can take to live in line with each of your values - what would make the biggest difference? For example, you may decide to reduce your air travel or stop eating meat as part of your value of protecting the natural world. Focus on these priorities to start with, then try to move all your behaviour in line with these values.
- **Pause and think before acting** - you don't have to think for several minutes before taking any action, but do just take a breath and check yourself before speaking or reacting, to assess what the impact of your action might be and what the best response might be. This is particularly important on occasions when you are inclined to react in an immediate, instinctive, emotional way, such as lashing out or shouting in anger. Just a slight pause can make a big difference to help you behave in a way that's consistent with your values rather than one you will regret.

- **Be honest with yourself** as to whether you're being consistent with your values or not, and then act accordingly if you're not. The most consistent response may not always be the easiest one, but it may well be the most satisfying in the long term.
- **Standing up for your values** - the thing about values is that the times where they are most important are when they are most under pressure and you feel it most difficult to hold on to them. So, courage is a key ingredient in our ability to stand up for our values. We need to get used to challenging and questioning things that instinctively don't seem right, fair or just to us, even if this just in relation to a minor incident in daily life (like asking someone to pick up a piece of litter they've dropped in the street) - as this 'practice' could give us the strength we need to stand up in the future when it really counts, if we are called upon to do so.

DEALING WITH CONFLICTS BETWEEN VALUES

Another issue that may have come up when you think about the actions you could take to live in line with each value is that an action that is consistent with one of your values may actually conflict with another value. For example, your planned action of visiting your relatives in Canada more often (to reflect your value of caring about people) might conflict with your value of caring for the environment (and the action of taking no flights). These potential conflicts can make people feel anxious or guilty because they don't know how to deal with them or feel they may have made the wrong decision.

Here's how to deal with it. When you see this type of values conflict happening, stand back from it and firstly look at the likely effect the action will have for each of the values. In this case, only you will know what the impact of going to see these relatives might be on your value of caring for people. The impact of the flights on the environment will be very large and negative for your environmental values though.

Once you've weighed up the likely impact of the action, prioritise your values – which of the values matter most to you? Which do you have the strictest rules for? If you prioritise the environment and are quite strict in your rules on it, then this may mean that you can't visit your relatives in Canada more often, unless you can find a more environmentally friendly way of doing it than flying. If you prioritise people above the environment you may decide to take the flights. Or, you may reach a compromise between the two – perhaps by taking far fewer flights than you'd originally planned. Sometimes compromise may be possible, but sometimes it may not, and one action may have to go.

Again, a healthy dose of common sense is needed in these decisions. There are no clear rules that set out how to live in line with your values. Just be honest with yourself about the impact you're likely to have and then make the decision. Often we make these decisions in split seconds in our day to day lives, but we can become better at making them if we follow the steps above.

LIVING HAPPILY WITH YOUR VALUES

The final point to consider in this chapter is how you can live happily with your ethical values.

Some people striving to live ethically can find themselves feeling guilty that they are not doing enough or feeling confused about how they should behave. This form of guilt can occur when someone is worried about whether a particular action is consistent enough with their values – for example, whether buying from a cheap clothes shop (and the possibility of sweatshop labour) may be inconsistent with their values about caring for people.

To deal with this situation, work out whether the potential impact of your action is likely to be big or small, and if it's big, decide whether you can make the time to do some more research about the impact to help your decision. In either case, make the decision then move on and don't give yourself a hard time. You've been through a proper thinking process on it and made the decision.

It's not always easy to live in line with our values so don't be too hard on yourself if you can't make the grade sometimes. However, you also need to be honest with yourself. And if you find yourself continually failing to meet the moral principles you have set yourself, and feeling guilty about it, then perhaps you've set your moral bar too high. In this case, you can either make more effort to uphold your principles or set the level of your rules lower and don't give yourself a hard time. So, be honest and firm but fair with yourself. Conversely, if you think you've set your bar too low, don't be afraid to try to set it higher and see if you can live by these new principles.

ACTION

LIVE IN LINE WITH YOUR VALUES

Once you've gone through the earlier exercise of thinking about what your values are, consider what steps you can take to live in line with each. Start with a few steps for each value, then add more if you want to.

WHAT DOES A MORAL SOCIETY LOOK LIKE?

Before we reach the end of this chapter, let us briefly look at another big question. We have explored the question of morality as it relates to our behaviour as individuals, but we should also consider how it relates to wider society.

We all want to see a better world. But what does this better society look like? What are the difficulties in achieving it? And how might we overcome these to achieve it?

First, we could argue that the question doesn't make sense. As we've already explored, morality is a made-up concept without clear parameters to it, so it's hard to put together a detailed definition of what a good society might look like.

Second, even though we set out a selection of values that many people might have in common, these are not all held in exactly the same way by everyone - so there may be differing opinions about what values constitute a 'good society'. Equally, there may well be disagreement about what we mean by each value. For example, do we achieve a 'just and fair' world by distributing resources more equally (as someone on the left of politics might believe) or by giving people the freedom to decide how their resources should be used themselves (more a view of those on the right)?

Not only is there a lack of clarity in the values themselves but also in how to achieve them. Even if we could agree on some specific values to overarch society, we could have plenty of disagreements of what political policies would actually achieve them most effectively.

All this shows that, if we thought individual morality was full of grey areas, societal morality is even more slippery. It is not realistic to hope for one single utopian society, as people don't all share the same vision of what this consists of, and some of the worst human regimes and tragedies have occurred because of people who've tried to enforce specific ideologies like this on societies.

So, what's the solution? Our current political systems are far from perfect but they are an attempt to do what we should be doing - having debates and ongoing discussions about these issues to reach a consensus about them.

One of our biggest current political problems however is that we seek moral certainty - about the 'right' thing to do, the 'good' society etc. When we hear political arguments, whether it is from people in politics or simply among friends, we usually forget that the moral basis on which people are making their claims and arguments is essentially made up, and that in politics, all we are really trying to do is negotiate different positions of grey. No 'right' answers exist, and anyone who says they do should be regarded with suspicion - yet, modern politics seems to be about trying to convince others that your position is 'right'.

Everyone involved in politics and seeking a better world would do well to remember the arbitrary nature of morality and of their views of how the world should be. This would enable everyone to realise that what we are really aiming to do in politics is have an ongoing discussion and negotiation on these grey areas, in a bid to find arrangements and rules that people generally agree on. In other words, to have a clear, honest conversation about the good society we want and how to achieve it. This process should be ongoing, because people's views, as well as the circumstances we face, change over time.

So, we should each continue seeking our own visions of a 'good society' but agree that this vision needs to be based on ongoing discussion and negotiation as a society, rather than the arbitrary moral viewpoints of a few powerful people.

SUMMARY

Morality is a made up concept - but as human beings, morality matters to us, both as individuals and as broader societies.

We each have responsibility for our own values, as well as setting how we'll live in line with them and monitoring how well we are doing this. Taking this responsibility is something that can give us a great sense of fulfilment in our lives and strengthen our sense of our own identity.

Once you've thought about your values, living in line with them may take some changes in your life and behaviour. But don't let this stop you from making the changes - if you want to live the life that's really you.

CHAPTER 11

HOW CAN I DEAL WITH DEATH AND GETTING OLDER?

How to age well — How to think about death —
How to think about other people's deaths

> *"Do not act as if you were going to live ten thousand years. Death hangs over you. While you live, while it is in your power, be good."*
>
> Marcus Aurelius

Human beings spend a great deal of time, anxiety and money trying to delay the ageing process, but getting older is something we all go through, and we need to embrace it as part of the rich experience of life, rather than a disability we need to fight against.

In this final chapter we will explore what it means to get older and how we can think about ageing in a clearer way, so that we make the most of each stage of life - no matter which stage we're at. We will also look at the subject of death, which is, alongside ageing, another certainty of life, and another thing that we spend a lot of time trying to ignore or avoid thinking about.

In looking at these big questions, we will also travel through some interesting topics that we might not have given much thought to before, including what the idea of time really means for us, and how change is a fundamental part of our lives.

It should be a fascinating journey, and one that helps you to make more of every stage of life, as well as to deal with the reality of death in a more considered and helpful way.

HOW TO AGE WELL

The aim of this section is not just to talk about old age, although this is an important area we will look at. We will talk about the idea of change and getting older in general - regardless of the age we are at.

This is something we all spend a lot of time thinking about in various ways throughout our lives - not just when we're in the later stages of them. For example, we might worry about how we're changing emotionally and physically as we enter adolescence, how to carve out a life of our own when we leave home in our early twenties or how our hair is falling out as we enter middle age.

WHAT DOES IT MEAN TO GET OLDER?

When we talk about getting older, we tend to mean one or both of two things:

- **The changing physical state of our bodies over time** - our maturing into an adult body, then the physical changes that result from moving towards older age, such as greying hair and reduced physical capacity.

- **The changing way we look at the world and think about our lives** - including our sense of the length of time we have lived, the accumulation of memories, our expectations for the future, how we view other people and how we feel we are viewed by other people.

We can't do a great deal about the first of these factors - the physical changes associated with getting older. We can of course take a number of steps to look after our physical health throughout our lives, such as eating healthily, exercising and not smoking, which will give us the best possible chance of better health later in life. But we can't escape the fact that we all go through physical changes as we age - this is simply a fact of life.

We spend a lot of time and money, both as individuals and as societies, striving to reduce the range and impact of the physical changes we go through as we get older, especially in old age - from cosmetic treatments to more fundamental health issues. Despite the significant advances we have achieved in human longevity and quality of life in our later years however, we are all going to have to deal with the physical changes associated with getting older.

We do however have more choice in how we deal with the second point above - how we look at the world and think about our lives as we get older - and this is the key area we can look at in the rest of this section. This includes how we think about the physical changes we're going through.

DEALING WITH CHANGE

A fundamental part of being able to age well is being able to deal with the idea of change.

Unfortunately, many human beings don't feel comfortable with the idea of change. We like certainty, and we're comfortable when things stay as they are. We can often see change as a threat – something to be feared.

But life is about change. We are not only constantly changing physically throughout our lives, but our outlook on life is constantly changing too, as we go through new experiences, think new ideas and find out new things. Even if we go out of our way to avoid doing any new things, the world around us can change our lives without us having any say in it – for example, being evicted from a home or a loved one falling ill.

Either way, we need to be willing to deal with change if we are to live well, and age well.

ACCEPT WHAT IT MEANS TO GET OLDER

Getting older simply means that our bodies and minds are changing.

We could choose to interpret this as the idea that our bodies are slowly wearing out, which is true after we reach maturity as adults. But we could also interpret it as the fact that our bodies are simply changing - and that change is not simply a process of degradation and a feature of old age but a constant feature in our lives, whether we're older or younger.

By seeing 'life as change' like this, we can have a more realistic view of our existence, rather than pining for a fantasy 'fixed state' that cannot continue for ever - whether it is of youth, perfect health or anything else.

REALISE GETTING OLDER IS WHAT YOU MAKE IT

We have a terrible attitude towards ageing and older age in modern society. The general view is that getting older implies decline - where we become less capable, less useful, less important and less attractive.

This attitude is harmful nonsense, as it is not only untrue, but it makes us view old age with fear and older people with derision - if we notice them at all. We need to change this attitude, particularly in a society where people are living longer than ever before, and older people are forming an increasing proportion of the population.

In reality, as we've noted, getting older is simply the ongoing process of change in our state - both physical, mental and circumstantial - as creatures. Each point in this process of change, whether it is aged 25 or 73, therefore has its own opportunities as well as disadvantages.

Getting older is commonly believed to bring ever-increasing numbers of disadvantages. Yes, we may slow down physically, have pain and physical issues sometimes and be unable to do some of the things we enjoyed before. But these disadvantages can be offset by advantages, if we choose to see them - for example, having a greater awareness of what matters to us and what we enjoy doing, caring less about what others think of us, valuing life and the minutiae of experience more and having more time (after retirement) to do the things we enjoy.

In short, we should aim to make the most of every stage of our lives on this continuum of change. Just as you are the author of your own meaning in life, you are also the creator of how you want to live and interpret your older age, so create it for yourself and don't let our society's negative view of it make you feel that either you or your life is less valuable as you get older. See ageing as change - not as decline.

ACCEPT WHERE YOU'RE AT

We are not in control of what much of life throws at us - whether it is ageing, balding prematurely or falling seriously ill - and we would improve our lives if we could release our tense, worried grip that attempts to control these things, and instead accept them and resolve to adapt to them and make the best of them (or anything) when they do happen. This doesn't mean we shouldn't try to do the things we can control - such as trying to prevent ill health by living a healthy lifestyle, or ensuring we take the steps we can to fight any illnesses we have. It is simply the idea of not burdening ourselves with jealousy, anger or resentment about our lives, and accepting them as they are.

10 MORE WAYS TO AGE WELL

Below are ten further ideas to help you get better at getting older - no matter which stage of life you're at.

1. **Be thankful** – whatever age you are, make sure you regularly remind yourself about the remarkable fact that you exist, and are able to reflect on your experience of life. As discussed in chapter 9, this is an easy way to maintain a sense of wonder about life, get connected with your inner world and feel more positive about daily life.

2. **Know yourself** – try to develop an honest sense of what you are really about, including what makes you happy and fulfilled, what makes you unhappy or uncomfortable, what your priorities are in life and how you really want to live. Don't judge yourself on your choices – just be honest.

3. **Be happy with yourself** - an important ingredient in your flourishing throughout life is learning to be happy with yourself, or at least accepting who you are. This includes accepting our natural tendencies, qualities and physical features and realising that we are neither perfect nor imperfect – we are just ourselves. It also means seeing the best in ourselves and making the best of ourselves.

4. **Keep fit** - it's important to keep both mentally and physically active throughout life. Taking regular physical exercise is good for you and makes you feel good. Keeping mentally active also has many benefits, so keep learning and taking an interest in the world around you - no matter how old you are.

5. **Keep connected** - the quality of our relationships with other people is one of the most important factors contributing to our well-being – if not the most important. Try to avoid loneliness and isolation, and seek to connect with others, as

even the simplest moments of connection – like saying hello to our neighbours - can make our lives better.

6. **Keep a sense of purpose** - having a set of interests, projects and activities can provide us with a real sense of purpose in life, which can in turn keep us feeling fresh and enthused by life. These could take any form, including helping other people, making things, fixing things, running a business or taking classes.

7. **Know your limits...** - as we get older, we may find we face physical limits that weren't there before - for example, back pain preventing us from playing certain sports. Work out which of these are genuine limits (and which of them can be solved), and accept any limits that emerge in your life with good grace.

8. **...and use them** - use your understanding of any limits you have in a creative way to think how you can add value to your life - perhaps by trying new sports or hobbies rather than the ones you were struggling at because of your physical limits.

9. **Don't lose your inner child** - keep your sense of curiosity, wonder, fun and enthusiasm for the world. Try to see life through fresh eyes every day, and it will keep you energised and give you fulfilment.

10. **Think of the present** - Looking back to the past too much can be a comfort blanket or a tie that stops us making the most of the present. Equally, looking to the future (whether it's with fear or expectation) too much can do the same. Don't burden yourself with imaginings. Make the most of the present.

HOW TO THINK ABOUT DEATH

Given that death is about the only certain thing about our lives, it is surprising how little we talk or even think about it. Although death is everywhere in modern life in the news, television programmes, films and computer games, we are largely shielded from the reality of death, until it affects us and people we know directly. In fact, it could be said that we spend most of our lives trying to avoid the subject of death!

This can be a problem, as we can be ill-prepared to deal with the reality of our own death, how to come to terms with it or even how to plan our preferences for arrangements around it. It can also prevent us from facing the reality of the death of friends and loved ones and thus make it harder for us to come to terms with it in a constructive way, or being able to help and support other people who need us at these times.

Often, when we do get round to thinking about death, it is with a sense of fear, panic or denial.

Being able to think about death in a realistic and courageous way is a critical life skill, as it could enable us to live fuller, better lives while we have the chance and, possibly, die better deaths. So, this part of the chapter explores some ways we could begin to contemplate the subject of death.

We will focus more on the idea of death than the practical side of how to deal with it, but charities such as Dying Matters provide comprehensive, accessible guidance and support on these more detailed, practical aspects of death – from how to support someone who is dying through to what to do when someone dies.

People have had many ways of thinking about death over the ages. Some entire religions could be seen as attempts to help people navigate the reality of death.

People have a range of different views about death, often influenced by their religious beliefs, including the idea of an afterlife. The following view of death is the most credible one we have with the information human beings have available - that death is the point we simply cease to exist as individual creatures and 'selves', and there is nothing after death. To understand why this is the most credible view, see chapter 4, on our beliefs and how we interpret reality.

It is time to adopt a more modern and enlightened view of death – without suspicion or fear, but understanding the reality of it and giving some thought to it throughout life, so that death is one of many areas of perspective that inform the way we live.

In this section we will examine a number of ways you can think about death – and life – that could improve your experience of both. It's also a good way to revisit some of the lessons we've learnt in this book.

And rather than starting by thinking about death, let's think about life.

1. APPRECIATE THE FACT THAT YOU ARE ALIVE

In earlier chapters we explored the benefits of regularly taking time to appreciate the fact that you are alive, and to savour the experience of existing.

This is a pretty fundamental activity in helping us to squeeze the most out of life, no matter how long each of us might have to exist. It gives us perspective, promotes a sense of gratitude for our opportunity to exist and can help us see our lives in a positive way, no matter what daily life might throw at us. Adopting this attitude throughout our lives could make it much easier to look back on a life well lived later on.

2. ACCEPT THE REALITY OF YOUR OWN DEATH

After about 80 years of living (if not before), you are going to die.

Just reflect on this fact for a moment. For it is perhaps the most important fact that surrounds our lives, yet it is the one that most human beings spend their lives trying to ignore or avoid. Indeed, many of the most popular institutions and ideas in human society (from hospitals to religions) could be seen as innovative ways we have come up with to avoid, deny or ignore this reality.

We can however massively enhance our lives by facing up to this fact and using it to ensure we live fully while we can.

It can be quite difficult for each of us to 'process' the idea that we are going to die, as our consciousness is so busy and our experience of life so vibrant that it's very difficult to comprehend that this will stop. We are so used to existing we don't think about not existing. But try to think about this for a moment, and let the reality of it set in.

Just to press this point home, consider the age you are now. Then, consider the fact that you're likely to live for a maximum of around 80 years (possibly way fewer than this) before you go through the final process of dying yourself. Do the calculations of what this means for you at this point in your life.

If this realisation of 'limited time left' hits you hard, then you are probably thinking about it properly. It's a sobering thought and is perhaps the starkest reality of life. But, for most people, it is obscured by our absorption in everyday life and the fact that death is a topic largely hidden from us in modern society.

So, when you find yourself sucked back into the so-called 'reality' of normal social life, and starting to feel that this insight and the philosophy on life that it leads to is a bit extreme, just remember a couple of things. You're only feeling this way because a) it is indeed a huge, possibly life-changing, thing to realise, and is the ultimate reality each of us lives our life in and b) very few people around you will have yet understood this – and if they have, some may not have accepted or faced up to it in the way they live their lives. So, be one of the select few who apply this perspective to their lives and see your life move on as a result!

3. SEE LIFE AS THE EXCEPTION, NOT THE NORM

When we die and our bodies stop working, our brains also stop working, and our consciousness and any memories or subjective sense of who we are disappears. Once your brain dies, any sense you ever had of being 'you' also disappears. Once we are dead, we don't feel a thing. And it is perhaps our consciousness – our feeling of existing – that makes it so hard for us to comprehend death. When you exist as a self-conscious creature like a human being, it is difficult to come to terms with the idea that we only actually live in this state for a very limited amount of time.

As individuals, it is easy for us to have a negative and doom-laden attitude to the idea of our own life and death. We often see our life as the focus point, and death as the end of it, where there begins an infinite period of nothing. Why can't we see it the other way? Rather than see death as the exception and life as the rule (i.e. death as the end of a life, and something to be dreaded), perhaps we should see life as the exception – a brief, but amazing flash of light – a window within the darkness of non-existence that we should make every moment of whilst we have the profound luck to appreciate the experience of existing.

So, an appreciation of the fact that we're alive can change the way we see death. This in no way diminishes the sadness of death – whether it's that of other people or our own. But it means that the sadness is limited to leaving behind all the wonderful things that came with being an experiencing creature, such as families, friends and loved ones, experiences and memories and being able to participate in life. This is indeed a lot to lose, but we can take solace from the fact that once we have died this will not matter to us and this regret will cease.

4. ACCEPT YOU'RE ULTIMATELY NOT IN CONTROL

The other comforting thing about our own death is that there is nothing we can do about it when it happens.

So, although it may be intensely sad to leave behind all the things that come with being an experiencing creature, if we can come to terms with the fact that we have no choice but to leave them behind, we can allow ourselves a more peaceful, fulfilling death. For some people this acceptance doesn't happen until near the very end of life, but it is part of letting go.

This is of course simply a general comment about the moment of death. And it doesn't mean that we don't have choice and control in our end of life care depending on how our life is ending – indeed, this sense of empowerment can be vital to our ability to have a 'good death'.

5. LET YOUR LIFE FLASH BEFORE YOUR EYES WHILST YOU'RE LIVING

A classic story from people who have come close to death is that they have seen 'their life flash before their eyes' in the moments before they were likely to die. This may give us the sense that each of us will have the chance for a final 'review' of our lives before we die – a chance to reflect upon the journey we've been on.

But not only does research suggest this is this largely apocryphal but the reality is that you may die suddenly and never get the chance to review the life you've led and cherish the memories you've accumulated. Life could end in an instant and we may never get the opportunity for a neat 'tying up' of our own narrative – which, for many of us, would seem deeply regrettable.

So, why not spend some regular time reviewing the journey of your life and being thankful while you are living? In other words, live "with the constant awareness that one's existence is not only finite but always in danger of ending unexpectedly."[54] It could make your life feel more enjoyable and fulfilled.

6. UNDERSTAND WHAT DEATH IS LIKE – TO HELP YOU DEAL WITH IT

Very few of us really understand what actually happens to people's bodies and minds when they die of some of the most common causes (such as cancer and heart disease), or what people (both the dying person and those around them) are likely to go through during that process.

But this could be an important piece of perspective and wisdom to develop and carry with us through our lives – not

54   Nuland, Sherwin B - How we die: reflections on life's final chapter, Vintage Books 2002, p.242

because of a morbid fascination about it but simply to help us understand the reality of the process so that our expectations are more realistic.

An excellent book to help you understand this aspect of life is "How we die: reflections on life's final chapter" by Sherwin B Nuland. As the author says: "Too often, patients and their families cherish expectations that cannot be met, with the result that death is made all the more difficult."[55]

This understanding can also equip us to make better choices for ourselves, and others, when we or they reach the end of life.

"Treatment decisions are sometimes made near the end of life that propel a dying person willy-nilly into a series of worsening miseries from which there is no extrication – surgery of questionable benefit and high complication rate, chemotherapy with severe side effects and uncertain response and prolonged periods of intensive care beyond the point of futility. Better to know what dying is like, and better to make choices that are most likely to avert the worst of it. What cannot be averted can at least be mitigated."[56]

7. UNDERSTAND WHAT DEATH IS LIKE TO HELP YOU TRULY LIVE

To help you truly live by understanding the reality of the processes we and our bodies may well go through when we die, we may well gain the final inspiration we need to convince us of the ideas discussed earlier – that life is a window of light in a sea of nothing, and that we should really resolve to live the lives we want, without letting it pass us by or burdening ourselves with unnecessary stresses and imaginings.

Death, when it comes, doesn't often take place in a way that we would see as dignified while we are healthy, and also often takes place in mundane, familiar places such as hospital wards, nursing homes and your own bedroom. What we're simply saying

55 Nuland, Sherwin B - How we die: reflections on life's final chapter, Vintage Books 2002, p.242
56 ibid.

here is that death is the ultimate leveller – so make sure your life that precedes it is better than mundane.

CONCLUSION – HOW SHOULD WE LIVE WITH DEATH?

We don't need to dwell on death as we go through life, but we should live with a clear sense of perspective at the back of our minds about how brief our lives are and that death is a certainty – however much it may be hidden away from us in modern society and however far away we may feel from it when we are in the process of living.

Having this perspective on death is just one of the many useful pieces of perspective we should be carrying with us in the back of our minds throughout life – others include our position in the universe, our situation and lives in relation to other people around the world. See chapter 2 for more details.

HOW TO THINK ABOUT OTHER PEOPLE'S DEATHS

We've just explored some ways we can think more clearly about our own lives and deaths. At some point in our lives though, we are likely to have to deal with the death of other people who are close to us. This may require some further thinking, but the perspective we have gained in relation to our own lives (and deaths) will help us here too.

1. ACCEPT THE POSSIBILITY OF IT

It is of course a major shock when anyone close to you dies, but at least don't let the possibility that they could die in the first place be a shock to you. What we mean by this is that, by having an acceptance of the possibility of the death of those we love at the back of our minds at all times, we can not only remind ourselves to make the best of these relationships while they're there, but also make it slightly easier to come to terms with these events if they happen.

Even considering this possibility can be a difficult thing to do, especially with our children or partners. This doesn't however have to take the form of a morbid obsession with the impending demise of our loved ones, but rather an acceptance of it as a reality of being alive, of the fragility of life and of having emotional connections to other people.

2. APPRECIATE THE RELATIONSHIPS YOU HAVE

We can use our acceptance of the reality of death, and the brevity of life (including of those we love) to remind us to make the most of our relationships and the time spent with people we love.

In short we should use our perspective on death to enhance our appreciation of life.

3. DON'T FEEL BAD ABOUT HOW YOU REACT

We all react differently to major life events, so the last thing you need to do during the testing time of dealing with the death of someone close to you is to judge yourself on how you're reacting compared to others and worry about whether it's the 'right' reaction.

4. LET THEM GO

If you are close to someone who is dying or whose life is threatened, challenge yourself to check that you are making decisions and giving advice that is based on what is best for the person and what they want – rather than what you want. That's why it is so beneficial when people make their wishes known before they are dying.

When we face the threat of losing someone we love, it can be extremely difficult to step back from our overwhelming desire to preserve their life and keep them around us, but try to make sure that you are thinking about it from their perspective.

5. TRY TO LOOK TO THE FUTURE

Being told of the need to 'move on' after a bereavement might seem to be a very cold and unrealistic idea, which completely fails to understand how the bereaved person may be feeling.

Despite this though, there seems to be some value in trying to accept the transience of things — even ourselves and the people we love the most — and using this to stop us holding on to anything too much — both people and anything else in life. This idea, used by Buddhism and several other schools of thought, can be very hard to follow as most of us cling to things in life — often quite naturally, as these things can give our lives meaning.

Perhaps though, it could help us to see other people as gifts that come into our lives that we don't own and can't hold on to forever. This in turn might make it a little easier to try to continue our lives making new attachments rather than letting the loss of past ones make our lives unbearable.

6. UNDERSTAND THEIR PREFERENCES

If someone is close to you and you may need to be involved in planning arrangements for them after their death (such as their funeral), try to make time to discuss their preferences for this with them in a calm and open way while they are alive. This not only gives them a chance to properly reflect on what they really want to happen but also gives you a good chance of meeting their wishes as closely as possible and with minimal pain.

FINAL THOUGHTS

Most people are reluctant to think about the topics of ageing and death, as they find them rather gloomy and lead to them facing realities they would rather not deal with.

We have shown in this chapter though that thinking about these topics in a considered and well-informed way can help to give us a new lease of life, regardless of what stage of life we are at. It can help us embrace life and be more appreciative of the time we have, as well as giving us a more helpful and perhaps more comforting perspective on death - both our own and those of other people.

Let's use this perspective to savour every moment of our lives and make the most of this unique opportunity to live them well.

"The greatest dignity to be found in death is the dignity of the life that preceded it."[57]

57   Nuland, Sherwin B - How we die: reflections on life's final chapter, Vintage Books 2002, p.242

FINAL
THOUGHTS

With the closure of death, we have reached the end of our exploration of ten big questions of life. The discussion has brought us back full circle to the overall view of life that we presented at the start of the book and have developed throughout it.

This is the idea that life is a brief flash of existence in an otherwise featureless expanse of 'not existing'. By adopting this view of life and death, we enable ourselves to see life as an opportunity to take as we wish, rather than death as something to be feared.

The aim of this book has been to show the value of a thoughtful and well-informed approach to life, as well as how to start living this way.

You now have a map to help you navigate the complexity of life. You can return to it if you ever lose your direction or feel you need to stand back and gain some perspective.

Good luck - and enjoy your journey!

FURTHER READING

WHERE AM I?

Docwra, Richard - Modern Life - as Good as it Gets?, Green Books, Dartington, 2008

Harari, Yuval Noah - Sapiens - a Brief History of Humankind, Vintage, London, 2011

Lloyd, Christopher - What on Earth Happened? ...in brief, Bloomsbury, London 2009

Rosling, Hans - Factfulness, Sceptre, London, 2019

WHAT AM I?

Hood, Bruce - The Self Illusion, Constable, London, 2012

Kahneman, Daniel - Thinking, Fast and Slow, Penguin, London, 2011

WHY AM I HERE?

De Botton, Alain - Religion for Atheists, Penguin, London 2013

Kneale, Matthew - An Atheist's History of Belief, Vintage, London 2014

Rovelli, Carlo - The Order of Time, Penguin, London 2018

HOW CAN I EXPLORE THE EXPERIENCE OF BEING ALIVE?

Blackmore, Susan - Consciousness - a Very Short Introduction, Oxford University Press, 2017

Dennett, Daniel - Consciousness Explained, Penguin, London, 1993

Heil, John - Philosophy of Mind: A Guide and Anthology, Oxford University Press, 2003

Nagel, Thomas - What is it like to be a bat?, Philosophical Review, October 1974

HOW CAN I FIND MEANING IN MY LIFE?

Baggini, Julian - What's it All About? Philosophy and the Meaning of Life, Granta, London 2005

Frankl, Viktor - Man's Search for Meaning, Rider, London 2004

HOW CAN I THINK WELL?

Davies, Nick - Flat Earth News, Vintage, London 2009

Docwra, Richard - The Life Trap, Life Squared, Lewes, 2018

Lakoff, George - The Political Mind, Penguin, London 2009

Levitin, Daniel - The Organised Mind, Penguin, London, 2014

Packard, Vance - The Hidden Persuaders, Ig Publishing, New York 2007

Schopenhauer, Arthur - The Art of Always Being Right - 38 Ways to Win an Argument, Gibson Square, London 2009

Zuboff, Shoshana - The Age of Surveillance Capitalism, Profile Books, London 2019

HOW SHOULD I THINK ABOUT OTHERS?

Cain, Susan - Quiet: The Power of Introverts in a World That Can't Stop Talking, Penguin, London 2013

Singer, Peter - Animal Liberation, Bodley Head, London 2015

HOW CAN I GET THE MOST OUT OF LIFE?

Csikszentmihalyi, Mihaly - Flow, Rider, London 2002

Docwra, Richard - How to Eat and Exercise Well, Life Squared 2017

Layard, Richard - Happiness - Lessons From a New Science, Penguin, London 2005

Russell, Bertrand - The Conquest of Happiness, George Allen & Unwin, London 1943

HOW SHOULD I BEHAVE?

Grayling, Anthony - What is Good?, Weidenfeld & Nicolson, London 2003

Leonard, Annie - The Story of Stuff, Constable, London, 2010

Singer, Peter - How Are We to Live?, Oxford University Press, 1997

Singer, Peter - Animal Rights, Bodley Head, London 2015

HOW CAN I DEAL WITH DEATH AND GETTING OLDER?

Grayling, Anthony - The last word on death
http://acgrayling.com/index.php?option=com_
content&view=article&id=54&Itemid=70

Nuland, Sherwin B - How We Die: Reflections on Life's Final Chapter, Vintage Books 2002

Becker, Ernest - The Denial of Death, Simon & Schuster, New York 1973

http://ideas.ted.com/2014/10/31/death-and-the-missingpiece-of-medical-school/